Tony Lake is a psychologist and Director of Wave-
length Communication Research.

Ann Hills, a freelance journalist, is a regular con-
tributor to the *Guardian* and editor of *Social Sciences*.

TONY LAKE / ANN HILLS

AFFAIRS

*How to deal with
extra-marital relationships*

A SPECTRUM BOOK

Prentice-Hall, Inc., Englewood Cliffs, New Jersey 07632

Library of Congress Cataloging in Publication Data

LAKE, TONY.
  Affairs, how to deal with extra-marital relationships.

  (A Spectrum Book)
  Original ed., 1979, has title: Affairs—the
anatomy of extra-marital relationships.
  Includes index.
  1. Adultery—Case studies.   I. Hills, Ann,
joint author.   II. Title.
HQ806.L34   1981   306.7'3'0926   80-21314
ISBN 0-13-018671-6
ISBN 0-13-018663-5 (pbk.)

Originally published as *Affairs: The Anatomy of
Extra-Marital Relationships* by Open Books Publishing
Limited, London, England. © 1979 by Tony Lake and Ann Hills.

10 9 8 7 6 5 4 3 2 1

Editorial/production supervision
and interior design by Eric Newman
Cover design by Honi Werner
Manufacturing buyer: Cathie Lenard

PRENTICE-HALL INTERNATIONAL, INC., *London*
PRENTICE-HALL OF AUSTRALIA PTY. LIMITED, *Sydney*
PRENTICE-HALL OF CANADA, LTD., *Toronto*
PRENTICE-HALL OF INDIA PRIVATE LIMITED, *New Delhi*
PRENTICE-HALL OF JAPAN, INC., *Tokyo*
PRENTICE-HALL OF SOUTHEAST ASIA PTE. LTD., *Singapore*
WHITEHALL BOOKS LIMITED, *Wellington, New Zealand*

Contents

Authors' note   *vii*

CHAPTER ONE
The forbidden subject   *1*

CHAPTER TWO
Marriage and myth   *13*

CHAPTER THREE
Ready for an affair   *26*

CHAPTER FOUR
First affairs   *47*

CHAPTER FIVE
Whether to continue   *63*

CHAPTER SIX
Why people cheat   *82*

CHAPTER SEVEN
*One-night stands
and multiple affairs*   *111*

CHAPTER EIGHT
Homosexual affairs   *129*

CHAPTER NINE
Re-awakening   *143*

CHAPTER TEN
The morality of affairs   *161*

CHAPTER ELEVEN
The realities of affairs   *172*

Index   *195*

Authors' note

All the case-history material in this book, with the exception of one letter published in a newspaper, derives from direct communication with the authors. Our grateful thanks go to all the interviewees and correspondents whose words are included, and also to Jill Tweedie and the *Guardian* for their permission to include the letter. Just as important in the preparation of the material were the scores of other interviewees and correspondents whose contributions formed the backbone of our understanding of extra-marital affairs. All the people who told us about their experiences had no more to gain than an opportunity to talk, and many had a considerable amount to lose. We wish to thank them for their trust and confidence.

We have, of course, disguised identities by replacing all actual names and places with fictitious ones, at the same time keeping as close as possible to verbatim reporting. It is just possible that our fictitious names and places may coincide with those of real people who were not interviewed and who did not write to us. We wish to emphasize that such accidents are the result of coincidence and are beyond our control.

May we also thank Patrick Taylor of Open Books and our long-suffering respective families.

AFFAIRS

CHAPTER ONE

The forbidden subject

FOR THE OVERWHELMING MAJORITY OF US, three acts in our lives are particularly public. The first of these is the announcement of our birth. Although the process of giving birth is a private activity, news of it is public property, and we each derive some benefit from this fact. The last public act is the announcement of our death. Somewhere in the middle, for a great many of us at least, we have our wedding. The main purpose of the wedding is to declare as publicly as possible that two people are now committed to each other in an exclusive relationship, come what may, for the rest of their lives. Like birth and death, the act is celebrated and then registered officially.

By contrast, the act of sexual intercourse is our most private social act. To carry out such an act in public is to offend sensibilities as well as convention. Yet it is not in itself a secret act, so long as the people concerned are married to each other. How, when, and how often they do it is their own business, but the purpose of their marriage was to confirm, for all to see, their right to carry out this act freely, in privacy.

An extra-marital affair, on the other hand, is a secret sexual relationship. It involves an act or series of acts of sexual intercourse that not only are private but that the two participants usually conceal by deceit. Either partner, or both, is married to someone else, and they are therefore not considered entitled to the freedom to make love as if they were married to each other. Unlike a marriage, an extra-marital affair has no public recognition and lies outside the recognized boundaries of acceptable behavior, both public and private. Yet, in their own way, affairs are just as much a normal part of everyday life as marriage itself. A major difference between affairs and marriages is that affairs are not acknowledged as something society can accept and debate openly. Why should this be so?

The explanation lies in the fact that, despite rising divorce figures, marriage is as popular as it ever was. On present trends, eight out of ten people can expect to marry at least once before they reach the age of fifty. Projections based on current statistics, though, indicate that approximately 40 percent of all current and potential marriages among women in their late twenties will end in divorce. Yet a great many will remarry. In 1975, about one-fifth of all divorced women remarried, and statistics also show that divorced men are three times as likely to remarry as never-married men are to enter first marriage. Remarriages after divorce accounted for nearly 25 percent of men's marriages in 1975, compared with less than 14 percent in 1960. As a society we seem to be moving toward more, but shorter marriages, not toward fewer marriages. It is not surprising, then, considering the popularity of marriage, that people defend it so vehemently. Part of this defense lies in the denial of the important part played in our society by extra-marital affairs.

A great deal of time and energy are spent defending the institution of marriage, simply by keeping our own marriages intact, or by helping other people to do so—whether as husbands or wives, as parents or children, or as counselors, advisers, and friends. Despite what most of us learned as children, people do not simply get married and live happily ever after. Their need to grow and mature does not cease. This frequently leads them in other directions and opens up previously hidden conflicts and differences. Their attitudes toward marriage and toward each other change. With these changes come deeper levels of conflict that, if the marriage is to last, may have to be resolved. One way of resolving conflict is for the partners to adjust their expectations of each other: Wives and husbands give up trying to change their partner's irritating habits, having decided that the survival of the marriage matters more. Many partners learn to accept that after a year or so of being married, or after the birth of a baby, it is natural for sex, which they once expected frequently, to become more routine and less impulsive. Wives who meet other wives become more inclined to discuss the intimate details of their partners' sexual appetites without feeling disloyal. The men turn more regularly to their colleagues at work or in the local bar, and discuss common difficulties. In this way, male and female expectations are discussed with relatives or with friends of the same sex, and support and reassurance are provided. Once the partners have harmlessly released the tension by talking things over with their own friends, they usually learn to cope with changes in their marriage.

Yet it is always a matter of degree. Some conflicts lie too deep to be resolved by such adjustments. Every individual resolution of a personal conflict can be a step away from the marriage. All the loving and sharing, all the excitement of marital unity at the start of the relationship, was based upon a voluntary, public denial of a certain amount of individual freedom. Part of each person was willingly suppressed and sacrificed to the marriage. That part may reawaken. Looking back at their early years, married men and women may wonder at the price of the sacrifice, and mourn for what was lost. After the first excitement cools, many of them begin to question the motive for the marriage in the first place, and wonder what they might be missing.

Traditionally, marriage means a pairing for life in a social, economic, sexual, and sometimes religious union. Many weddings are also a public declaration that two young people have arrived at full adult responsibility. They are ready to set up house together, to have sex freely, to bring up and provide for children. Traditionally, too, they have the strength of an extended family around them—all the aunts and uncles, grandparents, and cousins, as well as their own parents. In many societies a dowry system ensures for them the economic basis of a good start in life, and along with the dowry comes a guarantee of virginity, at least on the part of the bride. In our society, for all the differences between social classes, there are usually people at the wedding who will help financially, as well as bear witness to the public declaration of the contract between bride and groom. Church brides still tend to wear white to symbolize their virginity. All this is changing, however.

One major change is the fall in the number of church weddings. Civil-ceremony marriages are on the increase, and in many societies their number has surpassed that of religious-ceremony unions. Formerly, the traditional extended family was linked with many other similar families by a common religious observance. Marriages united these families not as strangers but as companions in belief. The public declaration made by bride and groom had a religious and a communal significance. It was harder for them to break their vows because the married couple was surrounded by relatives and neighbors who knew them. They were acutely aware of the damage that gossip could cause, and of the way their family, social, and religious standing would be hurt by their being seen to be unfaithful. Many people now choose not to marry in church because they feel that it would be hypocritical to claim membership of a community of this kind.

First marriages are declining in number, too. In 1960, fully 81 percent of men's marriages were their first, but by 1975 this figure had dropped to 72 percent. The proportion of women still single at ages twenty to twenty-four has gone up by one-half since 1960, from 28 percent to 43 percent. These trends have been noticeable for the last decade. Just because fewer young people are getting married, it does not mean that they are abstaining from forming partnerships. Indeed, the evidence suggests an increase, not a decrease, in sexual activity among unmarried young people. In 1979, the percentage of women aged fifteen to nineteen who were pregnant before marriage (16.2) had doubled from 1971. Today it is not unusual for a bride to be pregnant at the time of her marriage, although the proportion of premaritally pregnant women who married in the course of their first pregnancy was in 1979 half of what it was in 1971. Illegitimate births decreased from 67 percent in 1971 to 49 percent in 1979. However, they remain high among the younger age groups, and the decline in illegitimate live births is due to fewer births to women over twenty-one years old. About eighteen out of every hundred births are illegitimate. The traditional idea that the first marriage was also the first serious sexual partnership is obviously becoming obsolete, too.

Marriage as an institution is increasingly under pressure, for all that people defend it with great skill, determination, and understanding. Perhaps the most important change in recent history is the advent of free, effective, and uninhibiting methods of contraception, together with increased social and economic pressure to control fertility. Insofar as it need not lead to pregnancy, sex for many more people is no longer the gamble it used to be.

At the same time, there has been a revolution in attitudes toward sex as an activity justified by the pleasure it can give. This too may be becoming less of a lottery as more is known about the techniques that give pleasure. Orgasm has been studied scrupulously, and what has been learned is becoming more widely understood and applied all the time. Marriage as a sexual union has changed in significance partly because sexual union itself is understood better by more people. There is a more widespread recognition of sexual equality, too, in the sense that women are increasingly acknowledged to have the same right as men to enjoy sexual intercourse. Many of our grandfathers would have reserved this right for men only. It is a short step from here to the view that women should have the same opportunity as men to enjoy sex outside as well as inside marriage.

It seems likely that young married people today are not only more experienced with each other prior to their wedding night but also more widely experienced with others. Pre-marital sexual experience is more accepted, and it is also a means of discovering whether or not couples are sexually compatible, without running the risk of pregnancy. On the whole, it is argued, this should make for *better* marriages, not worse ones.

The extended family has declined in significance, as more families are scattered. When families gather together for a wedding, they see relatives on whom they have not set eyes for months or years. In the old days the traditional wedding was more of a day off for people who worked together than it is now; when today's wedding guests sit in church and listen to the couple take their vows, many of them are far more peripheral to the life of the couple than used to be the case.

These alterations in attitudes toward marriage and the family affect attitudes toward secret liaisons outside marriage. It is one thing, however, to accept changes like those brought about by sexual equality, easier divorce, and safe contraceptives and still believe in marriage. It is quite another to continue to believe in marriage and accept the universal and unfettered right to behave as though marriage did not exist. The revolution in sexual attitudes can only go so far before it becomes a direct threat to the fundamental structure of society. All societies are cemented together by some form of power structure, and our own relies heavily on the institution of stable marriage.

To illustrate this point, it is only necessary to glance through a magazine or spend an evening watching television. The family is still far and away our most important economic unit, a political pivot whose continued existence is still used as the most important incentive for production. This shows in the way advertisements are put together, wages are bargained for, and tax structures are arranged. The single population is constantly under pressure, from within and from without, to marry or remarry. Those who do not marry are still thought of as psychologically immature, economically selfish, emotionally eccentric, or merely born losers.

Despite the changes, then, people go on getting married and trying to avoid divorce. They try, as they always did and always will, to have happy, contented, fulfilled lives. If they find this difficult within marriage, most of them simply try harder. They do not reject marriage openly and logically and universally, but instead count their own experience as failure. To reject marriage as an institution would be to go too far. Few of us can imagine a society in which there is no marriage. Even those who are against marriage seldom feel that they have the power to change such a vast and powerful structure, however alienated from it they may be. So we defend marriage, and refuse to acknowledge publicly that extra-marital affairs are important. Each act of recognition of the importance of an affair forces people to confront their own doubts about the stability of their own marriage and of the society they live in. This also shows in the way people refer to affairs as "serious" or "casual." A serious affair is one that could lead to a new marriage. A so-called casual affair is often regarded as a piece of trivial selfishness, simply because it does not lead to a divorce and remarriage, however enlightening or shattering the reality of it might be for the participants.

Looked at from this perspective, the extra-marital affair takes on a different significance. It can be seen as a kind of necessary safety valve whereby individuals avoid confrontation with a major power structure and still manage to find ways of fulfilling the personal needs which that power structure would otherwise crush. At one level it can be a way of preserving the ostensible stability of marriage. Thus, articles in women's magazines openly ask: "Will an affair preserve your marriage?" Such articles argue that an affair can make you appreciate your husband more, or compensate you for the shortcomings in your sex life, making you fitter and happier, more able to cope with him and the children of the marriage. Such articles claim that affairs probably lead to the preservation of family and marriage—provided, apparently, that no one talks about it.

At another level, the psychological "power structure" that we all learn from our earliest days in our own family or origin usually sets conflicting goals. We were all taught to feel some guilt about our sexuality. Yet we also know how pleasant it is to be naughty and avoid retribution. Just as we needed that pleasure to compensate us in the face of the power of our parents, so in many marriages people can derive pleasure from beating the system through "harmless" sexual activity. The irony of cheating, the thrills of having a secret, the sense of power that comes from being sexually valued by more than one partner—all these feelings, and more, offer us safety valves at the individual psychological level.

Safety valves are useful devices for preserving a system when it is most under pressure. Not only marriage is under pressure; so is the family power structure. The extra-marital affair can be tolerated as a part of our society by most people, provided it remains a safety valve. To regard it as anything more than that—as a fundamental threat to the institution of marriage—would be something different. That would imply not a safety valve but a machine in danger of breaking down completely. So the existence of the affair and the extent of affairs are not things that people talk about. To do so would require them to accept the possibility of society without marriage—an unthinkable, unimaginable contradiction.

Accordingly, we act as a society to protect marriage. We accept it not only as the normal way to good sex, to births and family, to dignity in old age; but we also know how vulnerable it is too, how much work is required to preserve marriage in general and marriages in particular. Marriage is the acceptable face of adult sexuality, the

part we like to see, to which we are accustomed. Extra-marital affairs
are the dark side of sexuality, the bit we would rather not look upon,
that we know exists but whose implications we would prefer not to
discuss.

Once the whole question of the extra-marital affair is opened
up, it could inflict even more damage upon an already vulnerable
institution. If the contradictions inherent in marriage are unleashed
by public discussion, society might change beyond our comprehen-
sion. Would it not be better, we were asked when we said we were
doing this book, to let sleeping dogs lie? Marriage is hard enough
for people already. Why make their lives even more difficult? Would
we not do a great deal more good to society if we accepted that
affairs are meant to be secret, and are best kept as something
nobody talks about?

This is an argument that should be respected. Yet out of respect
for this point of view should come also an attempt to understand
the emotional and intellectual position of the people who put it
forward. What do they really mean? What are they afraid of?

Intellectually, the argument is an old acquaintance—that where
ignorance is bliss 'tis folly to be wise. Ignorance is such a poor
answer to most problems that it is highly unlikely to help in this
case. Affairs are surrounded by ignorance and by the companions
of ignorance: cruelty, insensitivity, and the denial of help to those
who need it. A better understanding of extra-marital affairs should
help to improve this situation.

The emotional position of people who feel that affairs in
general should not be discussed stems from the fear of insecurity,
and of the unknown. Almost certainly these fears are a reflection of
the need people have in a "married" society to feel that their own
parents were poorly married, and that being properly married they
stayed part of each other. Our parents' marriage, for all its inevitable
faults, was the fountainhead of our own lives. To threaten the
general concept of marriage is to threaten our own legitimacy, with
all that that entails. And it entails more for some of us than for
others, since a child who grows up within a disturbed marriage will
have grown more used to the conflicts of separation than a child of
a more stable marriage.

This is, however, only one of many emotions that are touched
upon by the subject of extra-marital affairs. At the general level,

people are as afraid of the insecurity of a society where there is no marriage as they would be of the insecurity of children deserted by their parents. But at the particular level—the level where individual affairs and marriages are discussed—many other feelings can be stirred up. It is the combination of all these feelings that makes people so fascinated by affairs.

Most people are fascinated to hear the details of other people's extra-marital affairs—provided the other people are distant enough from them. Eternally, this has been the staple diet of the gossips, and when there are not enough real liaisons the gossips are quite likely to invent some. Telling a secret to someone binds both together in a more intimate relationship. People who often know secrets, and let it be known that they know, are valued socially. They get attention because privileged information brings power. What is more, gossips have their uses. They are always in need of another juicy rumor, and will often pass on counter-propaganda just as readily as they passed on the original story that the counter-propaganda contradicts.

Rumors that link people in a sexual context have an extra fascination. They have given vicarious excitement to many a humdrum life. The fantasy is usually harmless, and the need (particularly of adolescents) to make up fantasies about other people's sex lives is understandable. But such rumors can have a devastating effect, particularly where they seem to confirm the worst fears of the implicated "innocent" partner—the wife or husband of the subject of the rumor, for example—or where they seem to imply a breach of a professional relationship.

Talking about the extra-marital affairs of people who mean very little to one can be a source of wicked pleasure and of innocent humor. Personal knowledge of the people concerned makes it a different matter. Some people take sides at once; others are slow to judge. Clearly there are several factors at work in this. Being closer to the problem can make people more aware of the complexities and more reluctant to ignore the contradictions.

If the affair has arisen as a response to an obvious crisis, the normal reaction is—whether you understand or not—to avoid making moral judgments and to try to help. Friends tell lies to help one another, providing alibis or professing ignorance. This draws them into the web of deceit that surrounds affairs, and, thus compromised, they are less able to take a moral stance on the issues of principle. The more obvious the crisis, the easier it is to justify such behavior. The less evident cases are the most difficult for friends to deal with, since they are easier to condemn but consequently more of a threat to the friendship. One of the social skills of life today is that of keeping one's friendship with people engaged in affairs of which one disapproves but that cannot be ignored. Perhaps it is also because more and more of us have direct and indirect experience of affairs, and do not wish this fact to be generally known, that the subject is so rarely discussed.

One further point is worth examining in this context. This is the problem of guilt by association. People who are prepared to stand up in public and talk about the subject of extra-marital affairs are inevitably suspected of having more direct experience than they care to admit. How do they know so much about it if they are not hiding something? If they declare their inexperience too insistently, they will be suspected even more. In addition, to talk on any subject is more difficult if it has to be a precondition that the speaker know nothing about it at first hand.

Yet it must be argued that society as a whole could gain from an open debate on the subject. Marital breakdown is increasing in a society that values marriage. The logic of this position is that we need a new set of widely accepted and openly defensible attitudes toward marriage. If it is not working, then the changes that are taking place should be openly discussed and our public apparatus adjusted to take account of private needs. Surely if more and more people are unofficially and secretly polygamous, then multiple marriages have a basis in fact that one day will have to be recognized in our law, social administration, and rites and customs. A deeper understanding of the nature of the extra-marital affair is an essential first step in such a direction. It is no longer sufficient to see the affair as just a passport from an unsuccessful marriage into a successful one. People have affairs not merely as a form of covert courtship that eventually and inevitably surfaces as a divorce from their first partner and marriage to their lover. Many have affairs as a form of multiple simultaneous marriage.

To understand the extra-marital affair, many questions have to be considered, in addition to the ones already raised. The most complex of these is undoubtedly why people have extra-marital affairs at all. In one form or another most of this book will be taken up with this question, and the main method used is the case study. People who were willing to describe their affairs in detail were interviewed, and the results are presented as a body of evidence from which generalizations can be made.

The question of why people have affairs is complex because of the many different levels at which it can be asked. The strategy used in this book is to start with some general issues and move toward more particular ones, asking all the time why people have affairs, but also looking at examples of different kinds of affairs at different stages during the affair. Why does an affair have to be secret? Is this an essential part of the motivation, or a necessary defense imposed on reluctant lovers to protect those who might get hurt? Are some of the problems faced by illicit lovers serious enough to warrant official recognition? What is the psychology of commitment, and are casual affairs where commitment is minimal less harmful or more harmful than serious affairs? There are many more questions to be asked, because there is no such thing as a "typical" affair. Like marriages, they are all different.

Affairs differ first of all according to external features. Sometimes it is the woman who is married, and the man who is single; other times it can be the reverse. *Singleness* can in practice mean separated, divorced, widowed, or never married. Affairs where one partner is married and the other single will be different according to the sex and the sexual experience of the persons concerned. In all these cases the secret is something that need be kept only from one marriage partner. In other cases both lovers may be married to other people.

Not all affairs, though they begin in secret, are kept secret. Some are discovered by accident. Other people disclose their affairs. This may or may not result in the break-up of the marriage. The motives for telling or not telling differ also. Telling about an affair can be a confession that asks forgiveness. It can also be a deliberately destructive and hurtful act. Sometimes accidental discovery is ignored by the "wronged" partner or partners. Sometimes people tell and are not believed.

Whether there are children in the marriage or marriages affected by the affair is often a decisive factor. In 1976, 43 percent of all divorces were between couples with children under the age of eighteen. Children are a shared responsibility that often keeps couples together despite extra-marital infidelity. Sometimes they are the reason why affairs end as secretly as they began. Perhaps, also, they are often the reason, superficially at least, why many affairs begin. Relationships can be fundamentally altered by the birth of children.

Yet another variable is the number of affairs pre-dating the affair in question. First affairs appear to have some characteristic features. Some wives and husbands who have had several affairs appear to increase their skill quite consciously as they gain more practice, and they take pride in the fact. The number of simultaneous affairs also varies. In some cases, one lover may be having only one affair. In other cases one or both partners may be having two, three, or more, all at once.

Add to this list the variable that is hardest to assess—the quality of the marriage or marriages concerned—and it is clear that no extra-marital affair is ever really typical. They are as different as the individuals who have them. However, the kinds of feelings experienced by the people concerned are often factors common to most affairs. There may be no defense against some of the worst of these feelings—jealousy in particular, that most destructive of emotions. The idea of sexual exclusivity is deeply rooted psychologically and socially, and it needs to be better understood by all of us— those whose job is to help the people damaged by affairs, and those to whom jealousy is an uncontrollable and obsessive scourge.

There is, in any case, no way of guaranteeing any marriage full immunity from extra-marital affairs. Sexuality is a most important aspect of all of us. It has long been thought wise by civilization that such a powerful force be controlled. Yet love has always found a way, and it has always been the best disguise for lust. Illicit love or illicit lust, the extra-marital affair has always been with us, too. But now we urgently need to understand it in new terms, and not merely to regard it as the dark side of our lives.

CHAPTER TWO

Marriage and myth

WHAT DOES MARRIAGE MEAN? Each marriage is an exception in some way to the general rule. The same is true of the extra-marital affair. Some affairs are undertaken as ways of obtaining those elements that the marriage is not providing. Many of these offer a kind of alternative marriage, sometimes giving a deeper and more sustaining relationship than the marriage itself. Yet the original marriage may continue alongside the affair, for many reasons. Other affairs are easier to understand as supplements, rather than as alternatives, to marriage; some of these provide the married lover with more opportunities to experience elsewhere the sort of feelings that the marriage already provides. In some cases this is an easy distinction to make. Sometimes, however, the two kinds of affairs—alternative and supplementary—are so intertwined that it is impossible to categorize an affair as one type or the other. To complicate matters further, in almost every case the factor that determines whether an affair is seen as alternative to or supplementary to a marriage is the point of view of the observer. The husband or wife who is having the affair may see it one way; his or her spouse may see it another way; his or her lover may take a very different view; friends, relatives, colleagues, and counselors may have yet another opinion.

Because every marriage and every affair is different, and because many affairs resemble marriages, it is far from easy to keep the differences in perspective. Almost anything is possible. There is, for example, the kind of affair that depends upon the stated or unstated encouragement of the legitimate wife or husband, despite the fact that this seems quite opposed to the idea of marriage. He or she may deliberately push the other partner into having an affair, and be equally likely to enjoy or to hate the results of the affair. A spouse may take the pressure off sex within marriage by suggesting that the other find a lover. A wife who took the decision into her own hands believed that "since I wasn't getting enough sex at home, it was a good way of preserving the marriage to have a sexual relationship outside it." The wife and the "other woman" are frequently found to be in collusion, because husbands have procrastinated about whom to choose. By contrast, some affairs, among them the so-called "one-night stands," consist of a very brief encounter, with or without full and successful sexual intercourse, and may either be forgotten within a very short time or remain in the memory for the rest of one person's life. There is no collusion because the spouse is never told.

Consider the following example:

When I was about fifty-five I was spending a week at a hotel in Madrid where I have a number of Spanish friends. I was out with them most of the time, but on the night of which I am going to write I planned to eat in the hotel. When I went down to the bar it was absolutely crammed with the guests of a Spanish wedding.

A very tall young man whom I had vaguely noticed in the hotel came over to me and asked me if he could take me over to the café next door for a drink, as there did not seem to be much chance of getting one in the hotel. I thanked him, we went, and over a couple of drinks we found that we were very sympathetic to each other. He was twenty-eight, a white South African, whose uncle, a poet, had lived in Spain and whose haunts he was revisiting. Eventually we returned to the hotel for dinner and never stopped talking! We shared many literary and other interests and our conversation seemed quite brilliant!

"You are a most attractive lady," he said, "and you have revolutionized my views on American women. You are old enough to be my mother, and I'm not the marrying sort, but if I were, I'd want to marry you." I purred!

After dinner we had coffee in the lounge and held hands. Going up in the elevator (our rooms conveniently turned out to be on the same floor), I remember looking up at him and saying: "You are a very tall young man." "Six feet six inches," he said, "and when did you know we were going to go to bed together?" "When did you?" I said rather weakly. "The moment I saw you come into the bar."

It was wonderful—passionate and gay and amusing, as a love affair should be. "Woman, you're insatiable," he laughed, and after my "deprivations" I expect I was.

He left at dawn and all he left me was the memory of a charming fellow, a perfect night, and a handful of small coins that fell out of his pockets when he took off his trousers. I knew his name and where he lived in South Africa. I suppose I could have tried to get in touch. It would have been a great mistake. It had been the perfect complete adventure and it was over. I shall always be glad and grateful for it.

From the woman's point of view, this was the perfect affair. On the other hand, however, consider the following report:

MAN WHO KILLED HIS MOTHER IS FREED

The nightmare of a man accused of killing his elderly mother after learning that she had been unfaithful with a milkman more than 40 years ago ended yesterday. S.J., aged 48, walked out of court after being cleared by a jury of the manslaughter of his mother, aged 67. He was sentenced to six months' imprisonment, suspended for 18 months, for assault, which he admitted. The jury, which was out for 40 minutes, had heard that Mr. J. had had a "violent argument" with his mother after learning that she had had an affair.

The court was told that his mother, Mrs. H.J., had

never missed an opportunity to criticize his father for a
wartime affair. This caused tension and misery in their
home.

Then Mr. J. learned from his father about his mother's
affair, Mr. J. told the police. In a statement he added: "I
thought it was terrible that my mother had herself been
unfaithful but was so intolerant of my father." He admitted
dragging her out of bed and assaulting her.

She collapsed and died from a heart attack, which, the
jury was told, could have happened at any time. (Report in
the Guardian, December 2, 1977)

In this case there were two affairs—the husband's wartime
infidelity and the mother's escapade with the milkman. Each of
these might have been a "perfect" affair in its own way for the other
person involved. Both Mr. and Mrs. J. knew about each other's
infidelity. Their son knew only of his father's affair. When he
learned of his mother's apparent hypocrisy in not admitting her
own sexual adventure, the son dragged her out of bed in a rage,
and she suffered a heart attack.

A comparison of these two stories—the Spanish adventure and
that of the bitter wife—raises several questions about the nature of
affairs and their importance. First, there are obvious differences in
the way the women in each story approached their own marriages,
despite the fact that full details are not given. The first woman only
hints at her "deprivations," but from the context it seems obvious
that in her own marriage she was tolerating a situation in which
she felt undervalued and sexually deprived. The adventure could
have been followed up. But, she says, "it would have been a great
mistake." She seems to have preferred the feeling of perfect satisfaction and reassurance as a way of keeping herself going in an
imperfect marriage, rather than taking the risk of ending her marriage and perhaps finding that her tall young man was not a real
alternative. The experience reaffirmed her individuality and
strengthened her resolve to persist with her marriage. The second
woman, according to her son's defense in court, said nothing about
her own affair, but never missed an opportunity to criticize her
husband for his, causing tension and misery in their home. Hers
was also an unhappy marriage—"a field of battle, and not a bed of

roses." The contrast lies in the way she apparently behaved, and in the reaction over a long period of both her husband and her son. Their family life was an open power struggle, with arguments designed to belittle one another, with the violence constantly breaking out, verbally and eventually physically. It was a thirty years' war. The woman in the first story used her affair as an inner strength. The unfortunate woman in the second story used it as a weapon.

The nature of an affair, then, depends not only upon what takes place in the illicit relationship but also upon how it is used in the marriage or marriages of the participants. Many affairs seem to be more important as part of a marriage than as a valuable event between the people having the affair. Certainly it often seems impossible to consider the affair without also considering the marriage or marriages involved. There are two separate questions to be asked: Why did this particular married person have this affair at this time; and how was the experience of the affair subsequently used within the marital relationship?

On the question of timing, it is obviously a mixture of feeling ready for an affair, and having the opportunity to go ahead with one when the right person comes along. But why do married people feel ready for an affair? What happens within marriage to provoke and foster this feeling? Is the nature of the marriage primarily responsible, or the personality of the "innocent" spouse, or that of the person who has the affair? If people feel ready for an affair, how far can they go without actually having one? Do these things just happen, or are they consciously or unconsciously engineered? Note, for example, the conversation in the elevator. He asked her, "When did you know we were going to bed together?" She did not reply that they were not, but asked "weakly": "When did you?" At which point had she decided? Could she have drawn back then, or had she gone too far?

Subsequent use of the affair is equally important and no less complicated. It is possible, for example, that the woman's affair with a milkman forty years ago may have encouraged her husband to have an affair subsequently, during the war. It is likely that the Spanish adventure was a similar restoration of the balance within a marriage. There can be no doubt that retaliatory affairs take place frequently: One partner has an affair. The other hears about it or guesses at it, and has an affair to make the score even. "I did not have any affairs until I suspected her of having one"; "She had an affair after ten years of marriage, but that incident awakened in me another world—from then on I had affairs, fast and furious," said two husbands. In the events that then follow, however, almost anything is possible. The partners may simply say nothing. Or they may tell and forgive. Or they may tell and not forgive. In any case there is every likelihood that the marriage will go on. What is it about marriages that means some survive many affairs on one side or both, and others do not? Why and how do some people tell, and others manage not to? What feelings are involved in redressing the balance, or in refusing to do so? How can some marriages continue when both partners seem constantly at war?

Before any of these questions can be tackled, it is necessary to take a closer look at what people expect of marriage, both as an ideal to be strived for and in practice, which often falls short of the ideal:

The first ingredient of the ideal marriage is love. The partners should love each other equally and so passionately so that for each, life would be meaningless without the other. Naturally this love is unique and exclusive. It starts with marriage and grows better over the years, maturing as the partners grow older. The idea of partnership is also vital to the perfect marriage—an equal sharing in the tasks of life. The sexual side of the ideal marriage is effortless and entirely harmonious—a touch, a caress, and the blissful couple explode in paroxysms of ecstasy. There is, in the perfect couple, perfect understanding, a kind of complicity that makes spoken communication scarcely necessary. The social life of the ideal couple is naturally perfect. They sally forth presenting a united front of harmony and good will. To all these qualities they add the apparently superfluous quality of persistence—they work hard to make the marriage work.

Although "ideals" like these are difficult to present in a serious manner, it is nevertheless true that many of these precepts are widely believed. It is certainly a common assumption that marriage works only if the two people concerned love each other. Yet a great many marriages persist between people whose relationship seems to most external observers to be anything but loving. The warring couple in the newspaper report quoted earlier is not unique. Many couples constantly grumble about each other, seem to fight like cats and dogs, and are uncomfortable together, yet they stay together, perhaps because they simply cannot imagine ever being apart. The ideal of love in marriage is often far removed from the reality. Unselfish love, constant and true, is probably impossible anyway. Nor does it help to strive for it, since forcing oneself to love someone is a contradiction in terms. Romantic love, in which one partner is placed on a pedestal and worshipped, is by today's standards of psychological knowledge not only ridiculous and dangerous but decidedly unhealthy. The current conventional wisdom is that only a very spoiled or neglected child could accept it, and only an eccentric adult could provide it. Love is beautiful and, like any beautiful phenomenon, is always more beautiful than a description of it or an explanation of its constituent parts. But if love has any meaning, then surely it includes the feeling of satisfying someone else's needs and having one's own selfish needs satisfied. It has only to fall slightly short of the mark to be revealed as essentially selfish.

Partnership, particularly loving and friendly partnership, is another ideal commonly associated with marriage. In practice, of course, the division of labor within a marriage is seldom equal, although the partners may falsely see it as equal, or accept happily the inequalities they know to exist. Many inequalities arise from an acceptance of traditional sex roles: the man as breadwinner, the woman as home-maker, and so on. Perhaps the most important element that binds people together in matrimony, however, is the economic factor. Two may not be able to live quite as cheaply as one, but there are economies from sharing, and people very easily become dependent upon economies. The family, including the married couple with no children, is an economic unit. It is fenced around with shared spending and mortgage agreements, and usually has its own internal monetary circulation system. To dismantle the economy of the nuclear family is no easy matter. The time, effort, and feelings involved in this aspect of divorce are far from simple. Partnership at an economic level may persist long after its loving and friendly origins have subsided, just because the effort required to take it apart is not seen as sufficient to justify the rewards of the available alternatives. Thus some affairs are simply not important enough to be worth the effort of reorganizing bank accounts and cash flow. Holy wedlock is often sustained by financial deadlock.

Sexual mythology about marriage abounds, as the tip of an iceberg of hidden feelings, sheer ignorance, self-deceit, and a great deal of social hypocrisy—much of it, apparently, more benign than malicious. Marriage is surely the only institution where sex without love and love without sex are accepted. The extra-marital affair that consists of sex without love is condemned. The affair that consists of love without sex is not seen as an affair at all. The "ideals" we depicted previously cannot possibly be true for all marriages most of the time. So why is it that people persist in attempting to achieve these ideals? It is a complex matter, and one that is at the center of the whole question of how, when, and why people have affairs. The case of Mrs. L. illustrates some of these complexities:

Often the persons most astonished by the result of an affair are the participants themselves.

Like many people of my generation [twenty-nine], I believed that sexual fidelity, while possibly desirable, was difficult, not to say impossible to achieve. I had long discussions with my husband about this before we were married, and he seemed taken aback but not opposed. I became pregnant immediately, and our physical incompatibilities were aggravated to a point where my poor husband was leading a practically celibate life. Prior to my marriage I had had two deep and fairly longstanding relationships, and a fair number of "fun" partners, so I was aware that for me our sex life was not great. However, I believe it is very much up to oneself to make it something special, and so I wasn't unduly worried about our marriage.

Unfortunately, I overestimated my husband's ability to absorb what information I tried to give him about my sexual turn-ons. The result was a progressive frigidity on my part, and I was relieved rather than upset when he eventually had girlfriends.

I would have preferred a *ménage à trois*, as it would have been the best solution, but he was appalled! Eventually I met a man some years younger than I was, while my husband was away on a business trip, and had a very exciting ten days. In many ways, I suppose, the pleasure I felt was out of proportion. But five years of frustration led to quite an experience!

When my husband returned he asked me almost immediately if anything had "happened." I said, "No," as it seemed the simplest way. Honesty is *not* always the best solution. However, I did not foresee how difficult it would be for me to hide the attraction between my other man and me, and within a week my husband became a changed man. He blamed me and the other man for destroying our marriage, and so on, and so forth, when he must have been aware for years that sexually it didn't have much going for it. It was in fact the old "I do as I like, but you do as I tell you!"

To give him credit, after a three months' separation he tried desperately hard to cope, but since I no longer wanted to have *any* sexual relations with him, we eventually split up. I completely underestimated the effect that good sex would have on my own acceptance of a sterile relationship, and I never expected my husband to react so violently when he realized I had been "unfaithful."

I have no doubt that I was naïve to believe that physical faithfulness should not affect a relationship unduly. However, I feel that had I been, had *we* been, more stable, it could well have proved an enriching experience. I still feel there are lots of delicious men in the world I would not like to pass up, given an option, but if I developed another "permanent" relationship I would approach an extra-marital affair in a rather different way.

At one level of analysis, the story in this woman's letter is a simple morality tale—"proving" that it does not pay to break the rules of the traditional marriage either (a) by rejecting the rule that married people should be sexually faithful to each other, whatever the difficulties, or (b) by rejecting the principle that they should tell each other the truth. She says she was probably naïve to believe that being sexually unfaithful would not affect their relationship unduly, and wonders whether the experience of the marriage would have been more enriching if they had tried harder to solve their sexual problem together.

Deeper analysis of the letter, however, points to some of the hidden complexities. Her response to the ideal of sexual exclusivity, in the discussions she had before they married, was to see it as

possibly desirable yet difficult to achieve. She eventually felt "relieved rather than upset" when her husband's response to her
inability to enjoy their lovemaking led to his having an affair. Her
attitude to the ideal model of sexual exclusivity comes across as an
honest attempt to admit her own fallibility. The standard of perfect
marriage was not one she felt able to achieve, nor one she could in
all honesty expect her husband to achieve. Perfection would be too
much to hope for. So she was prepared to accept a breaking of the
rules of marriage before she went into it. She was trying to be
realistic.

When her husband began to be sexually dependent on one
girlfriend, she took a further step toward a realistic solution by
suggesting that the girl move in with them. The *ménage à trois* was
an idea that horrified him. All this time she was having no sex life
herself but living up to the principle of the ideal of marriage—that
her husband should have a happy sex life—by accepting that he
had every right to love somebody else. It could be argued that she
showed admirable self-restraint, great generosity, and deep compassion. "My poor husband," she calls him.

Only after five years of frustration did she allow herself a
sexual affair. The resultant pleasure, she now supposed, was out of
proportion. But it showed her what she had been missing. As a
result she could not hide her feelings, and bit by bit during the next
few days her husband forced her to admit her infidelity to him. He
reacted violently, and they separated, had another try at making
things work, and eventually separated for good. She had underestimated two things: first, what she had given up by being limited
sexually to a man who could not give her sexual pleasure, and,
second, the extent to which her husband would react violently when
she stopped giving this up. Neither of these revelations seems to
have convinced her that marriage, or a "permanent" relationship
(as she calls it), must be based on sexual fidelity. Nor did her
husband's violent, irrational reaction stop her loving him or put her
off men in general. She wishes to love lots of men and be loved by
them. And she is honest enough to say so.

Yet there is another view, one that is altogether less generous
toward her. It could equally well be argued that when she married
this man she was setting him up as a victim of her own selfish
desires. She must have suspected sexual incompatibility, and, in-

deed, with her experience she should have known about it. Her discussions before marriage about not necessarily remaining faithful were clearly a preparation for the trap she had placed him in. She wanted a baby. Once she had the baby she would get rid of the husband. But she would do so in such a way that he would be to blame. So she became pregnant at once, refused him sex after the baby was born, and pushed him into a series of affairs. Not content with rejecting him and making him bear the guilt of his consequent infidelity, she wanted him to move a girlfriend into the house so that she could constantly remind him of her own self-sacrifice and virtue, rubbing his nose in the guilt every day, every night, in front of his own child. When he declined this opportunity, she waited until he was away, and then took a lover. The man stayed in her husband's house for ten days while they indulged in a sexual marathon—as often as not, probably, with the child somewhere in the house, confused and frightened, wondering where its father was and who this strange man might be. Then, when the husband returned, she lied to him. Small wonder he reacted violently. She clearly had not intended from the start to make the marriage work! Even when he tried to make things work after their first separation, she still rejected him. Her "realism" was merely a disguised rejection of the man she had vowed to love and honor until death. She could not cope with a real man, only with casual lovers and the baby. She still has no intention of trying to control her sexual greed. Next time she betrays a man she has sworn to be committed to, she will simply try to be a better liar so that she can have her own way on the sly, and not get caught.

Which is the correct view of her? Was she realistically doing her best to make her marriage work, or was she a hypocrite and a cheat pursuing her own selfish ends? It is impossible to tell. Either way, both of them—she and her husband (and, for that matter, their baby and at least two lovers)—were caught in the classic marriage trap: on the one hand the need to live up to ideal models of sexual behavior, and on the other hand the desire for sexual satisfaction. Few marriages, if any, avoid this trap. The faithful partners who know that sex is not working as well as it might have to make the best of the situation, and either suffer their "deprivation" in silence or find an outlet for it in the family power struggle. The erstwhile faithful partner who is tempted to try an extra-marital affair runs the grave risk of liking it too much and being permanently unsettled by it. The inner knowledge that good sex makes each of us come alive in new ways, that sex gives richness and depth to the meaning of life—this knowledge has to be suppressed in most marriages whenever love goes without sex or sex takes place without love. The suppression is painful to many, a denial of self-fulfillment, a deep loneliness and disillusion. If it is less painful to others, this may often be symptomatic of a "switching off," an escape mechanism that is expressed in moral authoritarianism, self-denigration, or apathy.

The general rules of the ideal marriage suggest that sex should always be perfect, and that it should express and maintain an ideal love. But who knows before marriage whether his or her partner is capable of this love? Without considerable experience of sexual intercourse together, which couple can be sure that their marriage will be sexually fulfilling? The marriage is supposed to last a lifetime. According to the ideal, each must adjust his or her feelings to take account of the reality that emerges. Blessed are those who expect the least, for they shall not be disappointed.

The traditional model of marriage offered a solution to all these problems. First, children were brought up to feel guilty about sex, and to be ignorant about what it might offer them. Second, they were expected to be virgins at marriage, and, since nobody said much about sex, it was comparatively easy to accept that what they experienced when they eventually experienced it was what it was supposed to be like. They could probably be tender and tolerant of each other's sexual failings, and, if they were lucky, love one another with the deep compassion of fellow victims of the same system. There was no need to worry about female orgasm. The wife simply did her duty and let the husband satisfy his animal passions. They did not discuss sex because nobody else did so. Third, if a couple were not suited to each other, they made the best of it. They hid their feelings. Those feelings that became too strong came out as violence or nagging. Married couples who beat each other or conducted a twenty-four-hour war of words were common enough. To be happily married was to win a prize in a lottery, and not everyone can expect to win the first prize. Fourth, the marriage was a social rite carefully timed to coincide with teenage puppy love and the achievement of social independence. Marriage gave many couples the consolation of independence from suspicious and over-bearing parents. Setting up house together was an adventure, a relief from arguments at home, a new-found freedom. If the love faded, there were the children to bring up instead. If the sex did not work, ignorance and guilt forced them to contain the problem, and to see their lot in life as normal. If it made them harder, less sympathetic to those—including their own children—who complained of wanting more from life than all this, then well and good. Their parents were no different toward them, so why should they not be hard too? Life *was* hard.

Hence the other rules of the ideal marriage. The partners do not let each other down in public. Each controls the other's sexuality. They must pretend to be perfectly adjusted. Each must persist; each must work hard at putting up with the price of being married. Love has to be worked out. It just comes naturally only for the lucky few. Friendship, finally, solves so many problems. Sex is not allowed to get in the way. It isn't all it's said to be in any case.

Of course, the ideal model of marriage is still with us. The defense mechanisms of society against the unbridled sexuality of its members are still seen as vital controls to protect our way of life. The idea that sex is selfish and love is selfless is the central myth on which this control is based. Like all effective disciplines, this one is also based on self-discipline. People have extra-marital affairs because they want them—for sex, for love, for satisfaction, as an act of rebellion, to spite their wives/husbands or their lovers, but always because sexuality will not be disciplined too far without adverse consequences: It will not rest content in chains. The motive to start an affair is always present at some time in each marriage. The opportunity may just come along, or it may have to be contrived, because life makes no sense at all without love, and more sense with sex than without it. Marriage is no guarantee of either, nor will it ever be. An extra-marital affair is no guarantee either, but it is less burdened with ideals than marriage and at least is not expected to last for a whole lifetime; and, if one is possible, more and better ones may follow.

CHAPTER THREE

Ready for an affair

IT IS PART OF THE MYTHOLOGY OF AFFAIRS that they are glamorous, exciting, and spontaneous. Here are two interviewees reflecting on their first affairs and their attitudes toward them:

> I began thinking about having an affair long before I ever took the first step, that is, actually went to bed with someone other than my husband. It was just a fantasy for a long time. He was away a lot, and one day someone, a neighbor I think, one of my girlfriends from the apartment building where we lived, said she knew for a fact that another of our friends was having an affair. I sort of said, "Oh yes?," and didn't pay much attention, but the idea took root, and I began to wonder, "Why not?" There was a good chance that Robert was getting it somewhere else while he was away—he was that sort of man. It didn't worry me, as long as he always came back, and I knew he loved me and belonged to me emotionally. It seemed such a glamorous idea, having a lover. There was no one specially

in mind, just a feeling that plenty of men would jump at the chance if I let them. Only I didn't let them, not for quite a long time. Then when it did happen, I wasn't ready at all, but it was great. (Janet)

All my buddies used to kid each other at work about getting an extra piece, a bit on the side. Guys like me who were young marrieds, particularly. The only one who said nothing was probably the only one who was having affairs. Nobody took it seriously. Half of them probably wouldn't know what to do anyway if they found themselves in bed with a real woman; a good-looking girl wouldn't look twice at them. They figured that all the married women were dying for it, desperate to get off while their husbands' backs were turned. But so far as I know none of them ever tried it. They were content to be "henpecked." I suppose my attitude at first was "chance would be a fine thing," but I doubt that I would have taken advantage as long as my own marriage was going well. There didn't seem much point. It's loneliness that makes you take the idea seriously, and married people can get lonely just the same as unmarried ones. (Brian)

Many men refer to affairs as "getting some on the side"—a pleasant adjunct to the plain fare of married life, not to be taken too seriously. The girls concerned are imagined as being sexually compliant, clever at anticipating the man's needs, always willing to do things their own wives would not do, and always desperate to see them. They are not insatiable, but to satisfy such girls is sufficiently difficult as to be a triumph, a proof of manhood. The grass, they say, is always greener on the other side of the fence. To be able to satisfy more than one woman is only part of their pride. To secretly possess something other men can only admire and lust after is an equal thrill. By having a wife and children to be proud of, a man shows that he is a fully qualified male, able to display his virility, and the fact that he is a normal adult. The addition of a mistress gives him the best of both worlds—the real world of full responsibility, and the fantasy world of the footloose and fancy-free, the stud, the lusty bachelor who can love them and leave them. To be available protects a man's pride in himself. So long as he keeps trying, he is a real man.

Many women have similar fantasies. Their lover will be a dashingly handsome young man, a "gigolo," perhaps, a well-endowed athletic type with a sports car. If he is not glamorous, he has to be rich. The fantasy is often that of the sugar-daddy, or of the milkman who wins the state lottery and says, "Let me take you away from all this."

Fantasies like these seem to thrive most where the opportunities are fewest. Most extra-marital sexual adventures may have their moments of glamour and excitement, but very few are truly spontaneous, if only because it is usually necessary to find a partner who is equally ready, and somewhere comfortable and safe from prying eyes where they can both go. These are not readily available to men with low-to-moderate incomes, who work regular hours and come home after work each day, who never go to conventions or stay at hotels, and who are easily recognized by other small-town citizens. Cars and local beauty spots offer some amenities, but impulsive, unpremeditated sex in a car requires considerable persuasive ability and a degree of practice and agility if it is not merely to be a sordid fumble. Nor is it easier for their wives. True, if they are housewives, they have the house and its bedrooms available during the day. But a low-to-moderate income has to be supplemented by wives' working except when children are very small, and to have small children in the house is an excellent inhibitor of unpremeditated sex with a stranger. The lover, whether or not he is a regular visitor, will be noticed by prying neighbors, and questions will be asked. Regular visitors—delivery men, meter readers, for example—will have other calls to make, and their visits will be watched and signs of movement monitored.

It is the better-off, the educated, who are seen as more likely to have the opportunities for taking a lover or acquiring a mistress. Obviously some are risk takers. One interviewee reported:

The type of woman I've found open is the middle-class mother with a couple of kids. She probably married young, was tied down young. She enjoyed her freedom after the kids started school, then as the children grow older she finds she has three or four hours a day of freedom, without the cash to go shopping. I am thinking of one particular suburb, where there was a group of a dozen such ladies I knew, quite attractive and with half a day a week to spare. Any smooth-talking fairly eligible man could create some kind of excitement in them. A crowd of us writers and actors thought we were fooling these women, but they were using us as much as we were using them.

Traditionally the only working-class sexual opportunists who actually succeed are traveling salesmen, soldiers living away from home, and sailors with a girl in every port. The tradition is probably untrue, but it emphasizes the problem of logistics. One male working-class interviewee argued that the circumstances he and most people like him lived under made an affair much less likely than the simple, casual sexual adventure:

I would define an affair as involving sex over some duration. About two years after I was married, I simply picked up a girl at a disco. I went there for a bachelor party when a friend was getting married, and I took her back to her home. I saw her once more, only. It made me feel guilty, but I justified it afterwards by saying it meant nothing. I lead a sheltered life, and this business just happened, rather than anyone taking the lead. I told my wife, but did not say we had gone to bed. I said I went out and got drunk. I had to say something because I did not get back until next morning. She asked me more, but I stuck to the truth with a few omissions. I think it would have hurt her if she knew—probably a sense of betrayal. At the time, I should imagine, she was asleep and did not worry. But it wouldn't have happened at all, except the girl had an apartment, and her roommate was away. There wouldn't have been anywhere to go, except where there was a risk of someone's seeing us. That's why I stopped seeing her, after the second time. Where I live it's hard to hide things, and unless you know a girl really well she probably won't want to hide things, so it gets back to the wife sooner or later. Quick sex in the back alleys isn't worth it, and to get bed-sex you've got to be lucky. (John)

Given that fantasies of lovers and mistresses are an escape used by many whose real-life opportunities for sexual adventure are severely limited, it is not surprising that extra-marital affairs are trivialized by descriptions like "a little bit on the side." Those for whom affairs are possible, and who look at the prospect realistically, are much more inclined to take them seriously, and to think carefully about their feelings before making themselves available or setting out actively to attract a new partner. Sometimes, perhaps, there is a sense of grievance about the marriage. But this seems to be less usual than the traditional model of marriage might suggest. More often there is a sense of loss, of emotional need. The man or woman who embarks upon extra-marital affairs is frequently coping with a sense of guilt, and is anxious not to hurt his or her partner. The feeling of being ready for an affair is often pushed back, suppressed many times, before it becomes more acceptable. Guilt and anxiety fight against the feeling of need. In a great many cases, guilt and anxiety are never totally defeated. The casual "one-night stand" affair that means nothing is sometimes an unconscious attempt to *fail* to meet a need, because the guilt and anxiety have actually won.

In my first affair there was no love, no rapport, just sex. It didn't make me feel any better. But it took a long time for me to realize. I imagine that's why I chose him. (Hannah)

It made me feel guilty, but I justified it afterwards by saying that it meant nothing. (John, quoted above)

Readiness for an affair, or a series of affairs, is generally thought of as being normal in men and unusual among women. Men are frequently categorized as being "after only one thing," and there is still a widespread belief that women are less interested generally in sex and more interested in being loved and cherished. To some extent this belief is now being eroded. It is slowly giving way to the view that there is a very similar range of differences between individuals in each sex. More sex education and the change during the last twenty years in the willingness of the media to publish serious articles on sex have probably encouraged this trend. During the 1950s, the Kinsey Report reinforced the traditional view that women were less interested in sex for its own sake, mainly because of the response given to questions about reactions to sexually arousing pictures. An explicit need for better sex, however, can be the starting point for a woman to begin an affair, just as for a man:

> I got married when I was twenty-one. Charles was sweet, and I always felt "safe" with him. I knew he loved me more than I loved him. We never fought, but I never felt mentally excited by him. I can't remember what we talked about. Our honeymoon was in New York. The sex wasn't too good, but the romantic idea was strong and I thought I was "in love." It was easy—he worshipped me and was kind and affectionate, and we were happy.
>
> After two years I realized I wasn't getting enough sex. I asked Charles to seek help, and he went to a psychiatrist, who said that Charles was still tied to his father's apron strings and wasn't ready to be a man. This was the cause of his "problem," premature ejaculation, and why he didn't want sex as often as I did. We could not afford the treatment, which was psycho-analysis. There are now several other, less expensive and probably more effective treatments available. I got pregnant, and having her [Annie] made us very close. But I stopped feeling maternal about Charles—he was very jealous of my breast-feeding Annie; he said it revolted him. That disappoint-ed me, but I loved feeding her. They were happy days. When she was six months old I began to feel sexually frustrated again. This time when Charles's brother began to make ad-vances I fought the desire but started to want to give in. He was very attractive and available, and I was bored and available and frustrated. Lonely in fact, but not angry. I began to tell myself that I wasn't getting enough sex at home, and that it would be a good way of preserving the marriage. There was no love, but I loved Charles, and I was starting to be a nag. His brother was a good talker, the mental stimulus I needed, I suppose. For months I believed it to be wrong and wanted to believe it would be right. It seemed best if there wasn't any love, just sex. That was what I missed most. I was turning into a vegetable, mothering Annie and loving it, mothering Charles and putting up with it, and sick to death of masturbating,

longing for the real thing before I forgot what it was like and just died inside. (Linda)

Some affairs are seen by their participants as having very much more to do with sex than with love; some are seen as having more to do with being loved, valued, and cared for than with sexual release. Above all, however, the extra-marital affair is an attempt by someone who is married to meet through individual, extra-marital behavior some personal objective, some private aim, that the marriage itself either has not met or has not radically altered. In this sense it is selfish behavior. It may often appear to make no sense when seen in relation to the marriage, yet it may make a great deal of sense in terms of the individual's emotional and personality development. This development, of course, begins long before marriage. It is rooted in childhood, grows through adolescence and pre-marital adulthood, and, despite the tradition that young men and women who marry should "settle down," it continues through marriage.

Part of the business of becoming ready for extra-marital affairs, then, is a psychological reassessment of the person's own private emotional objectives and achievements. Wives and husbands were people in their own right before they married, and part of almost every marriage is a willingness to limit private questioning about emotional objectives in favor of common development. In other words, what people actually join together when they combine in matrimony is their strategies for emotional development. They are still people with individual aims, who want to make sense of their own lives for themselves, but they have agreed to work together so that each individual will try to make sense of life above all in terms of each other. The extent to which this happens varies considerably. Some marriages seem to provide very little opportunity for the privacy of either partner from one another. Yet others give no privacy to one partner and a great deal to the other. In some cases the marriage seems to be a contract between two private people who remain private from each other, almost despite marriage. The extent to which a married person can still be happily or contentedly married while remaining a private individual, separate from his or her partner, depends on many factors. His or her own parents' marriage may have been very influential. The adaptability of the other partner in any affair must also play a large part.

A great many people who talk about their extra-marital affairs, however, give the impression that their individual emotional needs and objectives in life were not something they ever gave much thought to until they reached the stage of readiness for an affair. They entered marriage as a natural response to what seemed to be expected of them. As long as they could remember, growing up and getting married, then having children, was what everybody else did, and what they felt should happen to them too. For many, marriage is an escape from something—unhappiness of the parental home, the loneliness of early adulthood away from the home, the triviality of casual sexual relationships, the emotional insecurity of never being able to consistently relate one's own achievements to someone who cares about them. The situation that marriage alters may be so unbearable that almost any marriage will be a change for the better. Or it may be mildly negative, rather apathetic and purposeless, until the "right" person comes along and it all makes more sense with that person than it would without him or her. Then they try to make the marriage "work," and do not discover until later that they and their partner too, perhaps, were escaping from something else with which they still have to come to terms privately. To the extent that they are able to talk about this situation, and help each other understand the negative reasons as well as the positive ones for getting married to each other—to this extent they will grow together. However, the escape motivation may well remain unexamined and private. If people are unsure of their love, it can be very difficult to admit that a fundamental reason for marrying was to escape, say, an overbearing mother, particularly since this implies that almost any partner would do. Moreover, the overbearing mother—or, for that matter, the domineering father, the weak father, the spoiling mother, the deep emotional insecurity, and the lack of self-confidence that protracted loneliness brings—these negative influences, which the marriage seemed to be an escape from at first, do not disappear for long. Parents have to be placated still. The emotional insecurity tends to remain. Lack of self-confidence can be modified when the partner is there, and return when he or she is not present, at work or socially. Escape through marriage can often provide a new security, a breathing space for the refugee. But many a courtship does this too, and changes for the better that appeared to be stable and lasting in courtship lead to marriages in which the old problems emerge anew and unsolved to the extent that one or both partners begin to see the marriage not as a solution but as a mistake. This is often the point at which withdrawal from the mutuality of the marriage begins. A wife remembers:

> After the first child was born I said to my mother that it wouldn't bother me if I never made love again. The whole thing was overrated.

She found a lover and had an ecstatic meeting.

> I never forgot what it was like going home. I felt really unclean. I took a bath. I was certain my husband would know exactly what had happened. Mother—who had looked after the baby— would know, and the most guilt of all I felt was in relation to the child. I'd done something that was not acceptable. Then I thought, if I'm going to be doing this sort of thing it is no good staying married.

Her action forced consideration of lifestyle for the first time.

> I suddenly left my husband, and left a note to say so. I knew he would be violent if I told him directly. There was a period when he had agreed we should go our separate ways as the whole structure had collapsed. In the end he stopped me from seeing my son.

The myths about growing up play a large part in the way people see their own and their partners' emotional objectives. Romantic love, for example, is often based on an inner conviction that although nobody else gets married and lives happily ever after, they themselves are going to be an exception to the rule. Eric Berne and other transactional analysts have pointed out that many myths, legends, and fairy tales seem to act as "scripts" that the adult identifies with in childhood and tries to live out for the rest of his or her life. There is, for example, the Sleeping Beauty, who can be brought to life only by the love of one particular Prince. So many Sleeping Beauties marry their Princes, only to find they are not Princes after all. Then there is the frog who can be turned into a Prince, and the Cinderella whose Prince Charming rejects everyone but her after the ball, and who is rescued from oppression in an unhappy home just in the nick of time. People, he argues, cast about for a marriage partner who will play the various parts their scripts demand. They often end up being disappointed because their lives were based on fantasy, and the reality turns out to be very different.

At the heart of the traditional model of marriage lies a socially acceptable myth—that the development of the human baby intellectually, socially, emotionally, and sexually into full maturity should be more or less complete before marriage, and that getting married all but completes the process. All that remains is to finish it off and then have a new generation of babies. The cycle begins again for these babies, while the new parents, now complete adults, oversee the process and in their turn grow old gracefully. This myth, too, is now being questioned more and more. Part of what is being questioned is the reason for the social acceptability of the myth. It seems almost too conveniently to coincide with western society's ideas about when someone is old enough to be a wage earner, and, as a result, with our ideas about schooling and education. To study the way children develop is a useful exercise, since the results of such study can be applied in schools. To study the continued development of the adult after school-leaving age, into the twenties, thirties, forties, and so on, seems to have little applicability and is therefore less likely to be encouraged. But there may be a more important reason for people's willingness to believe that human emotional development is largely complete in one's twenties. This is that adults wish to believe it of themselves, and parents wish to believe it of their children. The former adolescent has tried for so long to be seen as a "grown-up" that nobody is going to be allowed to take that prize away from him or her, least of all older adults.

Yet although the myth that we are all grown up by our twenties, or even at the end of them, does not bear close examination, it is no simple matter to delineate the stages of development that most adults go through, particularly since there does not seem to be any clear biological sequence of development, except for menopause, which, around the fiftieth year, marks the end of a woman's fertile years. One idea is that there is a male equivalent of menopause. Another idea is that life between thirty and fifty often includes a "midlife" crisis in which the adult is more than usually vulnerable to a nervous breakdown and a loss of self-confidence.

What can be said with a degree of certainty is that the growth of the individual from childhood to adolescence is a progressive move away from direct dependence upon parents, but that for most of us this process is far from complete by the late teens. Parents continue to influence their children indirectly, even when direct influence ends. During adolescence they set the scene within which the child's emerging sexual autonomy is tested. Parents may resist or encourage adolescent sexuality, but they usually appear to attempt to control it by an extension of the same principles of self-control that they apply to themselves and that operate within their own marriages. This period can be seen as a struggle to establish friendship; and the battle waged by many adolescents to become accepted as individuals in their own right, as friends of their parents, is a direct reflection of the power struggles between the parents. Where parental power struggles are too fierce, the children may simply opt out, tired of being pawns in what they see as somebody else's fight, and go off to set up a power struggle of their own where they stand a better chance of winning.

Where the struggle is relatively mild, adolescents may join in on one side or the other, choosing girlfriends or boyfriends who are more acceptable to one parent than to the other so that the balance of power tips in their favor. Sometimes there is no struggle—on the surface or underneath—either because their parents are happy and harmonious or because one parent is no longer alive. With happy, well-adjusted parents, the adolescent or young adult is more likely to accept parental values without much questioning because he or she can contribute to their development. Challenges to authority occur, but these are absorbed in the friendship of parents and children. With bereaved parents, the adolescent is often retarded emotionally, and may become a part-time emotional substitute for the missing partner, delaying his or her own mourning for the death of the one parent by supporting the other during the several years of reaction after the loss of the other.

During the twenties, almost invariably, men and women set about the task of growing up by responding to the uncompleted sexual agenda of their adolescence. They attempt to meet the expectations of their parents—socially, intellectually, sexually, and occupationally—having determined during adolescence how to make sense for themselves of these expectations. They do it their own way, by a mixture of compliance, rebellion, and overreaction, but always in response to their parents. For many young men and women, there is now a double standard: what they think their parents would approve of, and what they feel is right whether the parents approve or not. The twenties are reactive rather than truly autonomous. Their parents are still too close and they themselves are too inexperienced for the marriage within which they grew up— their parents' marriage—to be seen in perspective. Conformity and rebellion are both likely to be overstated and extreme, perhaps in proportion to the fierceness of the power struggle that their parents went through earlier.

Most young people marry as an extension of this adolescent emotional development, with marriages that are a mixture of conformity and rebellion. They marry other young people who are going through a similar stage. As a result, many marriages begin as a conscious attempt to escape the worst features of the family of origin, but are in fact so much a reaction to the original power struggle that they are really alternative power struggles in their own right and end up repeating the features they were designed to avoid. Conforming marriages, wherein the partners are simply chosen to be acceptable to the parents, are particularly likely to imitate the family of origin. "I want a girl," goes the old song, "just like the girl who married dear old Dad." Whether the attempt is to conform or to rebel, many young couples are soon repeating the performance their parents staged some thirty years before. Their children repeat their own performance, too, by and large, since the new parents learned mostly from their own parents' lifestyle.

Some time toward the end of the twenties or during the early thirties, the next stage of development usually begins to emerge, with a reassessment of the achievements so far. In the contemporary nuclear family, most married couples have completed their families by this time. They are more used to each other, and are bound together by the children and by economics. Their own parents will by now have reached their fifties, and are less of a threat and more of a responsibility. The parents have usually accepted that their son or daughter is grown up, and that they have themselves become grandparents. Their own fertile years are over, and their sexuality can take on a new meaning for them or, if it never really worked, be set aside with a sigh of relief.

The thirties are generally less reactive and more autonomous years. In the traditional marriage—wherein the husband goes out to work and the wife has babies and stays at home—for the fortunate man these are years of steady consolidation at work, the promotion years. The man is young enough to want to do better, to show off what he can achieve, and to try to impress others who have more power. And he is old enough by and large to have appreciated the power of the systems that contain him, and to have seen the futility of constant rebellion. The woman has often had babies, and has become used to the idea of being mother and wife. She now has the same power her mother had over her in childhood and has to make similar compromises, similar social, economic, and intellectual sacrifices. If she has no career of her own, she may be more dependent than ever on her husband's occupational success and emotional stability. In such cases achievement may be measured solely in terms of the children, the home, and her well-being. For her these years are often not truly her own, as they are for her husband. She must wait until the children grow older. He cannot wait. But, although his successes are hers also, her successes (if they are limited to the home) often go unshared.

So to the forties. Traditionally, the man has used the previous decade to consolidate the gains of his youth, and at the end of this decade he will be middle-aged and slowing down. For many men it is a decade of regrets and attempted second chances. If he is unhappy at work, this will be his last chance to get out and start anew. If he is unhappy at home, these are the years of the search for lost youth. Yet in many ways, forty is a year of resurgence for the married woman with children. Her own mother, now at least in her sixties if she has survived, has to recognize this fact. The children have survived, are less emotionally draining, and take less of her time now that they are at school. She has perhaps ten fertile and mature years ahead of her. Intellectually and socially she is ready to grow again. If she attempts a second chance it will not be easy, but she often has the strength to try—perhaps resuming her former occupation, training for a new career, or re-emerging as a social power in the community.

It is the twenties, thirties, and forties that marriage dominates. Readiness to reassess individual progress through life increases, as the reactive twenties give way in men (and working women) to the more autonomous thirties and, in women with children, to the resurgent late thirties and forties. Early extra-marital affairs, those of the twenties, frequently reflect the conforming or rebellious characteristics of adolescence. To be ready for an affair is often an act of defiance, or of private reassurance, such as might have been played out only a few years before as a response to parental control or lack of attention. The marriage has taken the place of the family of origin, and reactions to it are similar to those learned earlier. The need for an affair may, however, arise from despair, from the fact that a reactive marriage is no longer working. Sometimes it leads to the end of one marriage and its replacement by another, more or less equally reactive. The extra-marital affairs of the thirties, forties, and fifties tend in general to reflect the traditionally different roles of men and women, and their different developmental tasks during these years, the years of "middlescence," the preparation for middle age. Often, however, they may be a reflection of delayed development, normal in itself, and just as much a part of growing up as going to school for the first time.

Readiness for an extra-marital affair may be seen by the person concerned either as a compensatory response to a marriage that may or may not be "working," or as a piece of private, individual behavior that does not concern the other partner of the marriage. However it is seen, it will tend to be a response that makes sense to the individual at the time. During the early stages of readiness for a first or second affair, however, the person who is married often attempts "trial" affairs, that is, extra-marital relationships that do not go as far as sexual intercourse.

I have a really good marriage, but I was working pretty hard at the time this happened. I'd spent three days in New York at a sales meeting, and all the false *bonhomie* started to get to me. It left a few rough edges, and I was missing my wife and the kids. I was also pretty worried about a few things, and suddenly felt kind of rebellious—ready to pack it in and run away. There was this saleswoman, attractive, fortyish, and I went out of my way to talk to her. She was very religious, too. We changed the subject. This impressed me, and I began to notice her properly. To make a long story short, we went for a walk and ended up in my bed—or rather on it, not in it. We just played. I felt no guilt at all, and neither did she. We kissed and tickled, and bit by bit we undressed. All except for her panties. She wouldn't take them off. We did everything else, even had an orgasm each, but no full sexual intercourse. She said that would have been "being unfaithful." I didn't ask whether she had even made love to anyone but her husband— it was obvious she hadn't. Later we slept and then made coffee and talked. We just talked out our problems—my worries, her marriage—and left as friends. That was the last night of the meeting and I never saw her intimately again. (Jeff)

This is not an extreme example of the way some people lay down ground rules for their conduct during the readiness stage. Another interviewee who had had several affairs told us:

If you meet someone and do everything but have intercourse, you feel happy, quite innocent. The point is not being found out. I don't think I want to get into any situation that would break up my marriage. I want to stay married at least until the kids are grown up. I'd like to find a girl who could beat me at chess. (Tom)

For many people, there is a very clear distinction between sexual activity short of intercourse, and full "penetrative" inter-course itself. This applies before marriage as well as to the extra-marital affair:

I first had intercourse at twenty-three but came pretty close with lots of men before, and went to bed with some of them. My true self is very sexual. It was quite absurd—if I had had intercourse with those men I would have been called promis-cuous, but as it was I didn't go all the way. (Gail)

During the period leading up to a first affair, doing "everything but have intercourse" helps people feel innocent, allows them to stay on the right side of irrevocable commitment. As Gail argues, there is often an absurdity about it. Two people may love each other, indulge in sexual foreplay in bed, even masturbate each other to orgasm, but do not count it as an affair because the "normal" sex act is not completed. Why is it not seen as unfaithful as full intercourse?

Adolescent training in the control of sexuality is probably the reason. During this period of development, many men and women become quite skilled at "heavy" petting, at "not going too far." They are acting this way in order to reconcile their own sexual needs with their parents' control over them. Because parents have forbidden full sexual intercourse, or warned them seriously about the dire consequences of it in terms of loss of self-control, the adolescent often goes as far as he or she can, short of full penetration. Later, when an anxious mother asks her daughter if she had gone "too far," the daughter can honestly say no. The same principle probably applies equally to the boys, but, whether it does or not, what a girl will permit her boyfriend to do is often the controlling factor and has ultimately more influence in adolescent sex than what the boy would like to do.

Readiness to begin being unfaithful to an absent husband or wife is often something of a replay of adolescent conduct for the person concerned. This time the spouse stands in for the parent. In early adolescence, merely to be seen holding hands may have provoked heavy criticism from some parents. Others would have looked the other way and felt angry but said nothing. Yet others would have smiled in friendly indulgence, glad that their child was happy. Later the adolescent begins to test more intimate aspects of his or her own sexuality, accepting an arm round the waist, kissing and cuddling, caressing of breasts, and then progressing to mutual masturbation. Adult sex-play goes through all these stages in a matter of minutes, compared with the more protracted exploratory sex of youngsters. With the adolescent, each stage was often subject to increasing anxiety about parental censure, and the triumph over this censure became personal victory for individual freedom over parental control. The adult who is near to accepting an extra-marital lover, instead of acting as a sexually complete adult, may often behave as he or she did in adolescence, progressively encountering more anxiety and guilt as the different, more intimate layers of sexuality are made available to the partner, and, in some cases, feeling progressively liberated with each step, and "open to new experiences." The interview with Gail illustrates many of these points:

My children are aged sixteen and ten. I had a good marriage from the beginning—very compatible. He is a good counterweight to me. I'm volatile, he's steady—almost too steady. He's an engineer—no high flyer, but successful, a high earner. He has not been unfaithful. His fantasy is a nymphet but his motivation is not strong enough to try.

Before I had an affair I thought about it a lot, and I talked it over with lots of men, trying to get their opinion. I would ask them, "What do you think about affairs?", trying to put it in a theoretical way. Without exception, every man would say, "Of course, I have affairs. The wife may guess but we don't discuss it." I realized that I was not alone. I did know of some women friends who were having affairs, but far more men. I think I was looking for social acceptance at my level, guilt clearance at another level. This still occupies me, especially the sociological angle. We are trying to create a new pattern that will move society away from conventional boundaries to new ones that I want to understand.

What I discovered was that it is important to follow one's own needs and instincts, to have one's own validity. I had this man—he was very fond of me, very involved. He had to get away from me in the end, because he really did want desperately to sleep with me, but would not. I said no on the first night we had the chance, and after that it never happened. He was getting divorced and did not want to get involved with a married woman.

I am available to new experiences, but I'm not looking. I only like complicated men. I find most younger men boring. I like to respond to something interesting. Intercourse has to be part of an involved, involving relationship. But I'm sorry I'm missing out by not allowing myself one-night stands. Men fall in love with me—I make them laugh.

Unlike the habitual marital partner, the new lover is often attentive and sensitive to each of these stages, more aware of the internal conflict, more appreciative of the cost involved for his or her partner. He or she may be happy to "settle for" a reassuring hand-hold, an arm around the waist, or other manifestations of puppy love that would in adult terms be brief stages on the road to full intercourse, because the tension of someone struggling against guilt and fear under these circumstances is evident and can be sympathized with and pitied. Moreover, after a long period of exclusive sex, people get used to the bodies of their partners, and find they need extra time to adapt to the feel of somebody new. This, too, has its counterpart in adolescent sexual behavior: The test of whether a potential lover really cares is whether he or she will wait until the other truly feels ready to go on to the next stage.

Although the restraints operating within the behavior of a man or woman who is not quite sure whether or not to begin having affairs are often closely related to the adolescent pattern of behavior produced years before by that person, the motivation for going ahead often relates rather more to the relationship with the absent marriage partner.

We just held hands. My husband never does that. (Woman, 53)

She seemed *interested* in what I said. (Man, 27)

He was very good, really. I just went on and on about Richard and the kids, about the complaints I had, just about my marriage. Then I said, I'll bet you're fed up with hearing about my problems, but I kept coming back to Richard, unloading it all. (Woman, 34)

What I couldn't get over was the fact she seemed to like me, and that she showed it. I was used to having my advances accepted, but not to having them appreciated. (Man, 36)

> We never stopped talking. . . . Our conversation seemed quite brilliant! ("Spanish adventure," quoted previously)

Within many marriages, in the words of one interviewee, "men have assumptions about whose body belongs to whom." His wife's body is his possession, a special thing that he owns, with spaces he alone is allowed to visit and to exult over. Little boys often feel a similar fierce possessiveness about their mother's body. The wives of such men are often closely bound by their own willing acceptance of this "little boy" element in sex. In the close intimacy of their marriages they share their man's exultation over exclusive possession, his boyish response to her bulk and warmth as he relaxes after ejaculation, snuggling close to her breasts, anxiety now gone, the little-boy look on his face, the maternal safety and comfort soaking into him from her. She may feel detached at this moment, closer to all women than to one man. She gives him the exclusiveness of having only one woman, as a boy knows there can be only one mother. At such moments the conflicts she may have with her man are reduced or ended because he is only a boy. In some marriages these maternal forms of love go on binding husband and wife together long after the wife has given up the hope of other consolations. They accept that their female bodies belong to their husbands in this special way, and that to allow another man into these spaces would deeply hurt their husbands, as a mother's rejection of her son is cruel and unthinkable. This is not an adolescent response but a maternal one. Perhaps the deepest sense of betrayal a woman can feel is when, after many years of marriage, she is widowed and has to face the prospect of allowing another man to own her in this way. For many widows, it brings as strong a feeling of guilt—perhaps a stronger one—as the married woman in mid-life may feel with her first extra-marital lover.

The story of Oscar, which follows, illustrates many of the points made in this chapter. He is now forty-four, slim, dark-haired, an attractive man physically. He has two brothers and two sisters and grew up, the son of a surgeon, partly in the town but also partly in the country. He went to a public school and university and is now the chairman of the board of a large company.

I had had two "girlfriends" by the time I was eighteen. I really had no awareness of how to get through to them other than with chit-chat and gossip about friends. There seemed no way to me of establishing a deeper relationship, although I am a very emotional person. I often wonder whether one's hang-ups about sexual matters would have been less later in life if one had had a certain ease, less reserve, not so much in sexual matters as when it came to expressing emotion and feelings about people in general.

During that second year at college—that was a good experience. It went on intensely for some time. Then she became engaged to someone else and I felt rejected. Then she broke off the engagement and we met a few months later. She had been in her final year and after graduating she traveled but became ill. The man concerned went back to India. I too had been traveling.

We remet and married. In emotional terms that first time around, other than sudden passions I had experienced as a teenager, I felt more strongly aware, more passionate than ever. Never the same after that, never so passionately emotional on my side again and probably not for her either. We had been apart for nine months—only nine months—and I had had sexual relationships in between losing her and meeting her again, sexual but not emotional. There was no question of any emotion. Obviously it was not the same thing at all.

It had happened then, and once since, that I caught myself looking for someone like her. This became an obstacle. It was like looking for someone the same but without her faults.

Our children were born two years after we were married and two years after that. We were well matched intellectually. I would say that the relationship deepened steadily over those early growing-up years. It was a good time. Nothing went wrong in the first few years. I had a couple of very small incidents after the first years. There was another time when I felt strongly for a visiting French girl, but it did not come to anything sexual. And I remember that my wife fell strongly in love with someone else, which caused a bit of a crisis. That was six or seven years after we were married.

Infidelity? Where the emotional commitment lies is more important than any sexual infidelity. When she fell for that man I remember being very upset indeed—about the sexual side. It was straight physical jealousy and a danger to the relationship. I can't justify it logically. It goes against my ideas. I remember telling myself that I should not feel that jealous, but it was there—jealousy even at the possibility. I have no idea if her relationship with the man was physical.

We discussed her feelings about the man. We later discussed affairs. With our heads we came to the conclusion that if either of us decided we should have an affair then it would be better if we did so. I thought we had agreed that if we had affairs we would not feel bound to tell the other. That was likely to cause more emotional distress. Later, however, I realized that she had not taken that in. The subject came up again after things had gone wrong, and I had had a couple of slight physical affairs. Other things had gone very wrong between us, and then I did fall very much in love with someone else, which complicated matters. One of the first things that came up in our frenetic discussions was that I had understood we would not tell, but she denied that. This was three or four years after *her* escapade. I don't know whether the marriage would have broken up without my affair. We have not gone into that yet. I have come to realize that the trouble between me and this woman—the fact that I had affairs at all—has been because of the bad things left over, left unsaid. I am aware of the danger that by improving the relationship with my wife things will be more difficult. Being committed to two people, emotionally. When things are relatively good I can concentrate better on what needs to be done. Just now I am somewhere near that state.

CHAPTER FOUR

First affairs

FIRST AFFAIRS ARE PROBABLY the most dangerous and difficult affairs of all. This is particularly true where the person having the affair is in his or her twenties, has not been married long, and was not very experienced sexually before marriage. For such people an affair is not only a fundamental test of their own marriages but above all a test of marriage itself. The young people concerned face a stark choice: Do they really want to be married or not? If they do, are they married to the right person? We shall explore the detail of these issues by looking closely at the stories of four people, whom we have called Peter, Dave, Rachel, and Valerie.

The characters

Peter is an accountant. He was born in New England, studied mathematics, and for the last six years has lived and worked in New York City. He married Sharon, two years younger than he is, seven years ago. They met at a dance at school, and she lived in a town some thirty miles away. Peter is now twenty-eight.

> Sharon and I got married very young. Her parents were against it at first, but they've accepted me now. My own parents didn't seem very interested either way. They came for the wedding, hardly spoke to anyone, and just left. We hardly see them.

Peter and Sharon have one child, a boy born three years after they were married. Sharon works part-time as a cook in a diner not far from her home. She is less well educated than her husband and, according to him, a rather shy person. It was not possible to interview her because she knew nothing about Peter's affair.

Part of Peter's motive for being interviewed was "to get it off my chest." Asked about his sexual experience before marriage, Peter said that he had had three girlfriends and had slept with two of them. He hadn't regarded those relationships as serious. He and Sharon had agreed not to have intercourse before marriage: "We were a bit old-fashioned, but we thought it was right." There had been a few "near misses"—petting that came very close indeed, particularly when they had spent a night together at her house with her parents sleeping in a nearby room. "The wedding couldn't come too soon for either of us. We were at it as soon as we reached our room at the hotel. A maid came to turn down the beds and found we'd not only beaten her to it but were actually in bed! We'd forgotten to lock the door!" Sharon was not a virgin, but had had intercourse only "once or twice before, at seventeen, shortly after leaving school." "We were very much love's young dream. We got an apartment and moved to New York when I got the job here."

Dave is a teacher, and he is married to a social worker, Liz. They have a large apartment in New York, and Liz is expecting her first baby. He is twenty-eight and she is twenty-seven. Dave attended a state college, and he met Liz during his final year there, as the friend of a girl he was "vaguely interested in" at the time. She has a degree in English and completed a course to qualify for social work. Dave teaches in an elementary school, and Liz is a member of a social-work team for a nearby hospital. Dave's parents are both dead—they were killed in a car crash just after he started college. He says he has gotten over it now, but he was numb for a year, and then "went crazy, sexually irresponsible," for a year. Dave's affair—

"my first and my last"—took place three years ago, about eighteen months after they were married. Liz said that she had had no affairs since the marriage, "but when I've got this out of the way" (her baby) she might! Dave's response was: "I dare you!" She immediately reassured him that she would not.

Liz's background is interesting in that her parents divorced when she was eight, and her mother remarried and was divorced again when Liz was at college. She feels she missed out in some ways, but kept in touch with both her father and her stepfather. "They get along quite well together!" Her mother is a "good friend" and "someone I admire." Dave agreed. Both Dave and Liz were going through a difficult period at the time they met. Dave was facing his final exams, having scraped through each year by the skin of his teeth. Liz was in love with a married man and trying to get him out of her system. He was, it emerged, one of her professors. "He really wanted to marry me. So you can ask me about what it feels like to be the other woman!" Liz and Dave helped each other— he moved in with her and they cooked, studied, made love, and studied. "He said if he passed his exams he'd marry me." "No, I said if I got a job we'd get married!" They lived together for about a year, and married in a civil ceremony "because I was pregnant— but we would have gotten married anyway." There was no fuss, and no honeymoon. They went to see her parents—"all three of them"—and wrote to tell Dave's married sister.

Rachel had three children before she was twenty-one. The first was a boy and the last two were girls. She was seventeen when she married, and her husband was then twenty-five. It seems to have been very much a dynastic marriage. Her father is an architect, and Barry, her husband, was an up-and-coming bright young architect, son of a friend of her father's, and her father's favorite employee. Rachel is now divorced, aged thirty-two, and the affair was one event that led to the divorce. The affair, with a man "almost twice my age," took place eight years earlier, lasted for nearly two years, and broke up his marriage also.

My parents never told me about sex. Even after three years of marriage and three children I hardly knew anything about it, but it didn't seem to matter. I was very much in love. My father wanted me to marry, and so did I, and my mother just told me to be myself and enjoy life. It was a very sheltered home. I did not have many friends my own age. Barry used to say he swept me off my feet.

Valerie is a nurse. When interviewed she was in the middle of a first affair and anxious to talk about it. She was twenty-eight and the affair had lasted four years at that time. She married a "businessman," Ralph, two years before the affair began, and had no children.

How the affairs began

All four—Peter, Dave, Rachel, and Valerie—talked about how and why they had started the affairs in question.

PETER

It was definitely due to difficulties in the marriage. We had been fine at first. We moved here when I got this job, and Sharon also found a job, in a drugstore. I was mad about her, rushed home from work, just loved every minute of it at first. We seemed to spend all our time making love. Then she got pregnant, and we had a few anxious moments over the baby before it was born. She went into the hospital twice, once for observation, and then for the last two weeks before he was born. Her mother moved in for a while. I got along with her all right, but I was also pretty fed up about things. Sharon had her hands full, and I said nothing about how I felt, just that I was all right. When the baby came, Sharon's mother went home. I did the nursing for two weeks, taking two weeks of my vacation. I used to love watching her breast-feed the baby. But it made a difference having the baby in the house. Jealous? Yes. It put my nose out of joint. Sharon said once that she was sick of my moping around the house and keeping the baby awake, and I should go out more and enjoy myself. I already was, as it happened. But I felt better because she told me to. I'd met a girl at a friend's party while Sharon was in the hospital, and I'd seen her once or twice for a drink on the way home from work, and bumped into her once at the supermarket. I liked her, so I decided to try my luck. She was a nurse, as it happened. She knew all about Sharon from what I told her. I knew she liked me. So I began to see more of her. It began to get serious when the baby was about three or four months old. I wasn't getting anywhere with Sharon. She'd let me, but I didn't want it that way. So I got more depressed, and said I was going out to a football game one Saturday afternoon, but went to see my nurse instead. Sharon knew I wasn't interested in football. The nurse and I spent the afternoon in bed in her house. She was on the night shift. It was stupid, really. We just went to bed, and had a good cry together, and made love, and then I went home.

DAVE

Dave's affair took place after he and Liz had been together for about five and a half years. He sees it as a kind of delayed reaction to getting married. At college he had been the local Casanova, at one time seeing three different girlfriends at once, and sleeping with a different one in rotation each night. All this had stopped when he met Liz. Of what led up to having the affair, he said: "I got itchy or something. Liz was fine. She worked long hours, kept busy and so on, but then so did I at that time—I was playing football after school, doing a play with the theater group, helping at a youth club. I just felt I was missing out in some way." He felt attracted to the mother of one of the theater-group kids. He'd told Liz all about it. The woman concerned was happily married and had two children. He hadn't told Liz she was happy in her marriage—he didn't know why. It didn't seem relevant. He has since told her. He didn't really know why she wanted the affair, except that she enjoyed sex and her husband didn't. Dave got into the habit of seeing her after school, while her husband was at work and her son was at Cub Scouts once a week. It was "mainly straight sex." Afterwards, when he got home, Dave said, he appreciated Liz more than ever. He felt no guilt about having started the affair. It seemed natural and it felt good.

RACHEL

She was twenty-four when the affair began. She had three young children, the eldest about six years old, and was living in Philadelphia. The children were no problem; she had plenty of help in the house and seems to have been bored. She could not describe a typical day, but it consisted mainly of finding plenty to do to pass the time. There were dinner parties in the evening to prepare for, she went to the theater, read a few books, dabbled at painting, and avoided things like housework and cooking. She took the children out, the oldest two to nursery school, and picked them up afterwards. Somebody suggested that she try writing, and she dabbled at that too. She says she was not really aware of having to do anything with her life. Her husband was her main concern after the children. Then someone put her name on a list to receive invitations to movie previews. She went to one or two of these, usually in the mornings. She felt like a terrible fraud. After one movie, she started talking to one of the journalists, and went for a drink. She thought nothing of it at the time, but she gave her phone number afterwards and said, "Call me some time." She felt amusing and witty and hadn't told him her name. He called the next day and they chatted for half an hour—"a long time on the telephone." She capriciously gave a false name and agreed to meet him. "I enjoyed having a secret, I suppose."

VALERIE

She married at twenty-two and the affair began "seriously" two years later, although she had been introduced to the man only a few months after her marriage. Her own family background was that she was the eldest of three children, whose father had cancer and had to have a colostomy. The children had been called together and told when she was fourteen. The father needed constant care at home. Valerie looked after him, taking as much of the strain off her mother as she could. She eventually became a nurse. She married primarily to get away from home, and against her mother's wishes, having completed much of her training as a nurse while living at home. She chose a husband as a deliberate part of this and had told him nothing about her father's illness. Her husband was a lonely man she had met through a dating service, a bachelor, then aged thirty-three. In the first year of their marriage they went on vacation to Italy and there met a couple who lived on the same street at home. Naturally, they got to know one another. The couple was also recently married—the man her own age, the woman, who had an independent income, much older. This man's wife became very friendly with her. On their return home, the friendship flourished and the four began to meet regularly for drinks and card games. The next year they went on vacation together as a foursome. That following Christmas, the man declared his love for her and the affair began. She started, she said, because she felt he needed her, because she felt very fond of him, because his wife seemed almost to be encouraging it. Her husband did not know and must never know.

During these first affairs, all four people—Peter with his nurse, Dave with his happily married woman, Rachel with her journalist, and Valerie with her neighbor's husband—faced four distinct problems. First, there was the problem of emotional control, both for themselves and for their lovers. Second, there was the danger of being discovered, and the question of whether or not they really wanted to be discovered. Third, maintaining a secret relationship places obvious but complex strains on the communication system between the lovers. Keeping in touch is difficult between meetings. Letters, telephone calls, and messages are all difficult to arrange so that the two can keep contact, and sudden domestic changes of plan or household emergencies may lead to one partner's failing to arrive at a rendezvous with no explanation. Fourth, each had to cope with the illicit partner's jealousy toward the official partner, with their own feelings of guilt, and with their vulnerability to emotional aggression from their lovers.

Emotional control

The dilemma facing the married person who starts an extra-marital affair, but who either does not wish to break up his or her marriage or is uncertain about his or her intentions, is how to prevent the affair from getting out of control emotionally. This is a dilemma because, on the one hand, where sex is involved, love is either a part of it from the start or is likely to be; and, on the other hand, he or she already loves somebody else and is married to that other person. Does the married person say "I love you" to the partner in the affair? If so, how passionately? If passion starts, can it be contained? And how does he or she respond when the illicit lover says those three little words?

PETER

Yes, I did love her. It began as sexual attraction, but it certainly became love, on both sides. I didn't say so first; she did, while we were making love together. I said it to her, too. It felt right to say it, and after that we said it often. I used to go home to my wife and baby thinking: Di loves me, Di loves me. Yes, I stopped saying it to Sharon, but I don't think I'd ever said it much anyway. But I was worried, because it got too serious. I hadn't wanted to get involved. Leaving her [Di] was agony, pure hell. Sometimes we just cried, held each other and cried.

DAVE

I decided not to tell her I loved her, whatever happened, from the start. Then she said she thought she was falling in love with me. I was a bit frightened. Liz and I never talk about being "in love." I'm not sure what it means, anyway. But when this grown woman started to say she loved me, the next step would be to tell her husband—and what a mess, I thought! We were passionate enough in bed, but mostly I enjoyed pleasing her, making her feel good. She liked my body more than I liked hers. She loved her husband too. I settled for—we settled for—the fact that you can love two people at once, in different ways. Later I began to get very attached to her, very fond of her. When Liz and I were on vacation I found myself missing her and sneaked a phone call. But it made me enjoy Liz more than ever when I went home after seeing her.

RACHEL

Neither she nor her journalist lover wanted the affair to become serious. She gave herself a false name, and concentrated on being pretty and witty, and on teasing him if he ever looked serious. It was she who took the initiative on the first occasion that they had sexual intercourse. She tried to make him fall in love with her, and began to succeed. He encouraged her to take herself seriously, to think of herself as a person with rights of her own and a brain of her own. She began to spend more and more time away from home, neglecting her family and old friends. Sex between them grew more obsessive, and she took to traveling across town to see him, "riding in taxis with my panties in my handbag." Rachel says she never tried to keep control. She found herself taking absurd risks. Once her lover came to see her at her house while Barry, the children, and the servants were all there. Fortunately, she answered the door, and the two of them made love just outside the house for fifteen minutes before he left and she went back inside. This happened about four months after their first meeting.

VALERIE

The affair between Valerie and her neighbor had begun with a declaration of love from the man. This had staggered her. At first she was totally unsure of her own feelings, and, although she felt fond of him and flattered by this attention, she also felt she was being disloyal letting a man other than her husband even think such things about her. "He said he didn't want me to do anything, or worry about it at all. He was asking nothing of me. All he wanted to do was love me from a distance." There was little she felt she could do. It was by now an established part of her married life that she and her husband went across to spend two or three evenings a week with their neighbors, and the neighbors came to see them on weekends. She was torn between telling her husband, and ending the relationship, and a desperate fear of loneliness if they stopped seeing the couple. Then, the following March or April, her husband went away on a business trip, and she had an argument with him before he left because she tried to arrange a trip away from home herself to avoid seeing her neighbors. "What have you got against them?" he kept asking her. She could not say, and when he left "I just stayed at home and wept." That evening, the man's wife came over to bring her over to his house, and she drank too much, the wife went to bed, and she and the husband made love. She felt disloyal, bewildered, and trapped. Her lover's wife seemed to know all about it, and, although the two women did not talk about the affair, Valerie felt some comfort from the fact that a man was in love with her, and that his wife approved: "She kept encouraging me to stay there." The wife would go to bed before Valerie left, after that week, and she and the husband made love. A bed was brought downstairs and set up conveniently for them. When Valerie's husband returned, she said nothing about the neighbors, and the old pattern of visits resumed—except that now on nights when there was no social call she used to slip across to see her neighbor's husband when the wife went to bed early. A code of light flashes was devised, and she took to watching the house from her own bedroom window. If the upstairs light went on while the downstairs light was showing, this meant the wife had gone to bed and the husband was waiting for her. As soon as the upstairs light went out she slipped across the street, often in her nightclothes. But she felt unconvinced that the man really loved her. Sexual relations with her husband ceased altogether.

As far as Valerie was concerned, her lover's feelings were not out of control, and she does not seem to have thought of her own feelings as being out of control either. In the interview she was asked what she and her lover actually did when they made love. She had some difficulty in answering, and said she was not sure. A pause followed, and then she said that he touched her briefly and got inside her. That was all? Yes. Did she join in? Yes. Another long pause. Did she touch him? No, she had never done that. She had very strong inhibitions about sex. Did she enjoy sex with her lover? "Yes. Yes, I suppose so." And with her husband? *"He* seems to." Did she feel loved? "Yes. I feel loved, but I don't know what to do."

Discovery of the affair

Peter says that he did not want his affair to be discovered. However, as he and Diana, the nurse, grew more and more fond of each other, they began to develop a make-believe scenario for the future. She said she wanted to marry him, and he found himself agreeing. They went for walks and looked at houses. When he got home to Sharon and the baby, he began to pick faults and argue about them. Sharon grew more depressed, and their marriage seemed "headed for the scrap heap." Several times he nearly told Sharon about the affair, but he was afraid of hurting her as deeply as this would have done. He found himself hoping she would find out, and became bolder about being seen out with Diana. Once Diana wrote him a passionate love letter that he kept in his jacket pocket for weeks, but Sharon never found it. He had her photograph in his wallet. She never asked why he was out so often.

Dave, on the other hand, "knew from the start" that he was going to tell Liz. He thought about how to tell her, and decided to wait until the affair was over, and then tell her. He was more worried about the possibility that his lover would tell her husband, or that the man would find out by accident and become violent. His lover was becoming careless, saying she didn't mind if he found out, that it would do him good, that she despised him anyway. He discouraged her from finding out exactly where he lived, but she found out anyway. What at that time did he think would be Liz's reaction? "I thought she'd be very angry and hurt, but that she wouldn't leave me." He took no risks at all of her knowing until he was ready to tell her. "She knew me too well." He meant that if she had the slightest suspicion she would jump to the right conclusion. She would have "scratched the other woman's eyes out."

Rachel courted discovery. When she described the risks she took, she seemed to be saying that she wanted to be found out. Yet a lot of the thrill for her was in living dangerously. In the interview this was tested by asking whether she took precautions to prevent a pregnancy, and she said she had not really taken care consistently. She did not like the pill, and used a diaphragm with her husband, and sometimes her lover used condoms. She gave the impression of wanting to have her lover's baby, and she admitted to fantasies about this. Her lover's family was nearly grown up. She had never met them. Her lover had told his wife that he was having an affair, and that it was important to him.

For Valerie, discovery seemed almost perversely unobtainable. She knew that her lover's wife was condoning the affair, and eventually, when the foursome were on vacation together again, she and his wife began to talk openly about it. The discussion centered on the idea that Valerie should leave her husband and "retire" to the country as part of a threesome. There would be no money problem. Valerie was not at all ready to leave work as a community nurse, however, and she had agreed only to think about the idea. As for her own husband, he simply did not inquire. She was slipping across the street at all hours of the day and night, often naked under her coat. Her husband said nothing. She was asked if he must have known, if her lover's wife could have told him. There was no way of knowing. It was more important that other neighbors did not know than that her husband might find out. In the interview she gave the impression that her husband was impotent and that her lover's wife was menopausal and asexual, and that she pleased all three—her husband by being undemanding, her lover by being compliant, and her lover's wife by keeping her lover sexually satisfied. They were all using her to suit their own purposes. This was suggested to her, and she agreed. But what did she want for herself? She said she did not know, other than just to be happy and make others happy, to be loved; but then they all loved her in their own ways. Discovery—making the complicated system she was trapped inside an overt system, not a secret—would have made little difference unless she wanted it to stop, since all the actors in the drama seemed to know all about it, but did not want to talk about it. The *ménage à trois* would have meant leaving her husband, and she felt she could not do this.

Communication

During an ordinary day, a man and wife make many simple decisions about how they will spend their time. One or both have to go to work at certain times, and usually come home at regular times also. There are chores to do, such as shopping and cleaning, picking up things from stores, contacting relatives, and so on, that must be done from time to time, but to which a less rigid timetable is applied. After the more or less rigid discipline of work times, and the slightly more flexible scheduling of chores, there is time left over for leisure. Most couples decide together what to do with this time, and have only themselves to please. In many marriages, one or both partners have separate interests outside the home—organizations they belong to, meetings to attend, or friends they see singly. It is generally recognized that domestic emergencies, minor or major, take precedence in deciding how this time may be used. For example, if one partner has made an overt arrangement with somebody else, it can easily be broken, either because he or she will understand or because an acceptable excuse or white lie can be told. When one partner is having a secret affair, however, the clandestine arrangements are covered by a lie of some sort. Domestic flexibility is harder to retain, because when an emergency blows up, or when there is simply a change of plan, the lie that has been told to cover up a meeting with a lover has to be tested. "Why don't you just call up Jimmy and say you can't come?" is very difficult to answer if Jimmy does not exist, and is really Joan, and Joan cannot be reached by telephone.

PETER
I used all sorts of excuses to get out to see Di. Football was one. I used to say I was at the game. Trouble was, Sharon used to ask me not to go and I had to pretend I'd be letting my friends down. Then she said she'd like to come, and I said we were pretty rowdy and she wouldn't like it. Then I said I was helping the bowling team at work. Or helping a friend move furniture. After a while she left me alone and got used to my excuses. If for any reason I couldn't get away it was sheer murder. Di said she'd understand, but she gave me hell once because the baby had a temperature and I couldn't get away. There was no way to phone her—just a pay phone at the apartment. When things like that happened, I used to stay later with Di and that made things worse with Sharon.

DAVE
No problem, because Liz was always home later than I was anyway. My girlfriend found it harder. Her husband came home early once and she hadn't been able to let me know, but she pretended I was a door-to-door salesman and I got the message. At the height of the thing she went through a period of hanging around outside here [his apartment] and Liz once asked if I knew her. I'm a good liar, and she says she never guessed.

RACHEL

"Phoning him was difficult, particularly if his wife answered the phone, or one of his children. We used to talk in a kind of code, and if his voice changed I guessed there was someone with him, and sometimes I said outrageous things to provoke him into being sexy or saying he loved me." At first they made complicated arrangements about meeting. Later they seemed to meet anyway, without discussing where or when. When arrangements broke down they both accepted this and did not resent it.

Jealousy toward the official partner

Except in the case of Valerie, where no information was available, the unofficial lovers seemed to have been through a period of quite deep resentment of their partner's spouse. Peter's nurse was deeply attached to him, and wanted to be his wife. He, in turn, felt sympathy for her, and could understand these feelings, but was still very reluctant to agree when Diana criticized Sharon. "Toward the end it must have been clear to her I wasn't going to leave my wife, and she spent a lot of time crying. I stopped talking about Sharon, because it made us both unhappy."

Dave, on the other hand, seemed rather insensitive to this issue, but the episode when his lover kept "hanging around" outside his apartment suggested that she had become very emotional, and Dave agreed that she "probably" resented Liz. Rachel talked about this aspect of her own first affair in some detail:

I wanted to be his official wife. I was very proud of him. He was a beautiful man, honest and talented, and it disturbed me that she could go anywhere with him and be accepted as though he was hers. I think he felt the same way about me. . . . When one loves a man, one wishes to be seen with him officially. The little things matter—being accepted as family, being able to phone him at work, being with him at Christmas and birthdays. It mattered so little to her, and too much to me.

Summing up

First extra-marital affairs, like those of Peter, Dave, Rachel, and Valerie, place a particular strain on the marriages of those who undertake them, because emotions can so easily get out of control. The affair often begins as a private adventure, a response to individually experienced needs that the married partner feels unable to share with his or her spouse. At first it may be justified privately as not being important, but, if it becomes important, then there is no one with whom to share the personal crisis that so often follows. The joy has to be contained; so does the pain. For a married person, to end an affair can be utterly devastating, yet the grief and the sense of loss must be contained privately. Trust, in so many marriages, has to be absolute, because the married couple are so interdependent emotionally. To tell about an affair, even after it is over, is to admit to having betrayed absolute trust, which, once destroyed, can never be rebuilt.

PETER
In the end, I went to Diana and told her we'd have to end it. It had gotten too serious. We agreed, and didn't see each other for nearly three weeks. It was purgatory. Then we nearly started again, and I came the closest I've ever been to breaking up with Sharon. I psyched myself up to tell her. Then, at the last minute, I thought: You can't do this to her. Even now I could never tell her. She trusts me.

Where trust is not absolute, a married couple may still have a deep, loving, emotional commitment to each other. Dave and Liz were asked if they trusted each other.

LIZ: I don't think trust is everything. Of course I trust you to stay with me, so long as you put me first. We're right for each other, aren't we?

DAVE: Yes. Besides, I've grown out of all that, now. It was not something I'm proud of.

LIZ: Being married is a kind of contract, but it works, not because of holding someone to their side of the contract,

but because in the end there's nobody else who's right
for you in quite this way. I believe in the chemistry of it.
Sex with Dave will always be the best sex I ever get. I
envy other women who get it from him, but he'll always
come back to me. I hope. He's the only one I ever want.

Commitment, however, is inevitably to the unknown aspects
of a marital partner as well as those that are known. As a marriage
progresses, the partner may be revealed as having characteristics
that are unacceptable. While the married person feels that he or she
has no choice but to live with this, the problem is contained. But an
affair with somebody who turns out to be more suitable undermines
this relationship. Rachel said: "That first affair would never have
worked as a marriage. We had terrible fights at times: we were
incompatible. But he never put me down the way Barry did. I found
out I was undervaluing myself because Barry undervalued me."

First affairs are tests of the individual marriage, but they also
test the idea of marriage itself. They seldom arise spontaneously:
For most people the commitment to marriage, the familiarity with
a husband or wife, and the nature of domestic organization in most
households help to prevent spontaneity outside marriage. By the
time somebody has decided to take an opportunity that creates an
affair, he or she has also, usually, privately decided to try behaving
like an "unmarried" person. To some extent it is an attempt to see
if they like being unmarried again. This can be because they feel
they did not complete their adolescent sexual agenda, that they
missed, or are missing, something other people have. They may
well have their fling, like Peter and David, and return to the fold
again. Or they may resume their sexual development, and regard
the episode of marriage as a chapter in this larger story, as Rachel
did. For Valerie, at the time of her interview, neither her marriage
nor her sexual development as an adult had really begun. Perhaps,
though less dramatically, this is what happens to many people.

CHAPTER FIVE

Whether to continue

WHEN AN EXTRA-MARITAL AFFAIR STARTS, it may well be a potential new marriage. This is, of course, not always so. Some affairs are deliberately lightweight, more a sexual adventure than an affair. But when an affair becomes serious, what should be done about it? There seem to be several alternatives—to continue and not tell, to tell and continue, or not to continue at all. Early or late in marriage, to carry on and not tell indicates a significant move away from marriage. The result may be the establishment of polygamous marriage, a polygamy in which at least one wife or husband is unaware of the arrangement. Or it may be a postponement of telling, a way of keeping open the option of a change from one marriage to another for the partner concerned. Not to continue at all is the alternative that traditional morality would require. In the experience of many men and women, this has simply not proved possible. A fourth option—not to continue, and to tell about it—is sometimes as bad as telling and carrying on. This is what happened to "Margot," whose letter was published as part of Jill Tweedie's *Guardian* column (May 28, 1978):

I was married twenty years ago to a man who was vital, witty, sometimes charming, but often vicious and violent. Halfway through the marriage I fell in love for the first time—with a man who treated me with gentleness and respect, rather than criticism and abuse. I therefore felt that my affair, which lasted four years, robbed my husband of nothing we had ever had.

The break-up of this relationship caused me to have a mental breakdown at the end of which I confessed my long-standing "misdemeanor," hoping to establish a more honest and mutually rewarding marriage. The news shattered my husband. I achieved nothing except bitter, vehement outbursts, informing me that I had no idea what I'd done to him by my confession, that he had had many chances to be unfaithful but had thought it wouldn't be right.

Finally I decided to sue for divorce and now I have been informed on good authority that my husband had had at least three affairs before he ever found out about my infidelity.

Tonight I asked him if he would have preferred to never have known, for my liaison to have been conducted discreetly, without any rocking of boats. His answer was an unequivocal yes. He also says that I am the odd one out in wanting to know the truth always, however much it hurts. He says I am asking to go through life exposing myself to pain. Perhaps so, but especially in marriage, shouldn't relationships be built on trust and honesty?

The issues involved are very personal; they depend entirely on the person or persons concerned, and on their judgment of the state of the marriage and their own needs for their illicit lover. Nor, in practice, does the age of the people concerned, or the length of time they have been married, make a great deal of difference. With a longer-established marriage there may be special factors—the fact that an older wife who is divorced, for example, may feel that she is less likely to find a new partner simply because she is older. This, incidentally, may explain why more men than women remarry after divorce. But then younger wives, with children to look after, face a similar problem. They are equally a "drag" on the marriage market, as computer-dating companies have long recognized.

To illustrate some of these difficulties, two stories are presented. Both show how difficult it is within marriage to tell and continue, and not to tell but still continue. The ages of the two people who are central to the stories are very different. One is sixty-eight. The other is thirty-two. The first is a man, the second a woman.

GERALD

I could never take friends home—my father worked at home and so friends were not welcome. I don't look back on boyhood much as a great part of life. I had T.B. from the age of ten into late adolescence, and I think it was because of tension at home. It would have made a difference if I could have taken other kids home. I envied boys who could follow that normal life. I could go to other boys' houses but not invite them back. When I had my own children I had the ordinary parental worries about their choice of friends—but they brought them home.

Girlfriends? That was the time when girls and boys did not develop young, and it was very rare for them at school to have friends of the opposite sex in any loving relationship. I did not start being interested in friendships with the opposite sex until I started working. I was getting $45 a week. In those days the boy paid if he took a girl out, so you had to have money to do it. Not until you were going steady did the girl share expenses. It is very different now. You were expected to have a girlfriend and be with her. I did just that. The idea of having intercourse before marriage was just not considered. I can remember one guy I knew. We used to go camping at weekends—all very pure. This guy brought a girlfriend along, took her into the woods, and screwed her. The rest of us could just not do it. We were horrified and very indignant at any suggestion that we might be jealous. We just didn't see things that way.

I married in 1938 at the age of twenty-five. We courted. We were going steady for two or three years. I met her through work. Then after a year of marriage I went into the Army. But for most of the war I wasn't far away—had a boy born in 1944 and a girl in 1946. There were a couple of "ships that pass in the night" during the war. Things that just happened, grew out of social life at the time, a U.S.O. party, any excitement. It was part of the atmosphere of the time, I suppose. Although I was not all that keen on keeping up with the boys, something I knew could happen given the opportunity. It wasn't for me. The first was a girl I met at a party. She was quite interested in having a man that night and had not been averse on previous occasions, though I hadn't pushed it. The other was the wife of a man serving abroad, and was desperately lonely and anxious for some sex. You can say that neither was wholly without love.

I had a moral stance in relation to intercourse, but only because of my wife. From her point of view she could not accept the fact that there was a sexual relationship outside marriage, though we did not discuss details. That was the background she had been brought up in, much more religious than mine. She would have been upset if she had known all about these occasions. Later I told Clare [the woman with whom he had the main affair] about them. I could be much franker and share my thoughts with her. She had much the same educational background as my wife, but is fifteen years younger—my wife is the same age as I am. Otherwise there was not much intellectual difference—only in the way intelligence was applied.

About Clare. She was a work colleague. We met in 1960. It was a close social relationship. My wife liked her. She was accepted as a local friend. She was attractive, but she had no boyfriends in any sexual sense. She was a virgin. From her point of view, I guess, she was prepared to wait. She came from a very sheltered background. I would not have thought she had many opportunities to rebel. The job was her abiding interest; she was popular, good company. She left the place where I worked, and got an even more responsible job. Almost as soon as the work relationship ended, the sexual one started.

I don't think she said, "Stop putting your hand there" or "Let's make a conscious decision." It was something that consequences and decisions forced. The sexual relationship developed over five years until 1970, when the problem became unbearable. We got to the point where we went on vacation as a threesome, but my wife did not know the truth about us. On one occasion I slept with my wife and then with Clare in another room. We liked each other's company. Admittedly it was a diabolically dishonest way of carrying on—not that different, I imagine, from other extra-marital relationships. As our feelings grew stronger, we had to come to a decision.

Judged by present-day standards, the marriage had not been all that satisfactory. There was not a lot of shared excitement. Sexually it was not very good, but I did not have anything else. You made your bed and lay in it. Opportunities for anything else were limited by legal and financial constraints. Life was not impossible, but it could have been much better. It would have helped if my wife had had more contact with people of her own age and interests. Just looking after a home and using the media for seeing the outside world is not enough. Of course I had fantasies—thoughts that it might be better with others. But the actual change arose out of an office contact, as I said. Clare was working with me, living nearby, she had her own apartment—all major factors. We had a working relationship that developed into a social relationship with the family for a few years—I left my job and went elsewhere, but still in the same city.

In the end, I made the break around 1970 because Clare said we can't go on like this: The affair was serious. It seemed that more and more people were aware of the relationship. There would be a blow-up and inevitable gossip. I had planned a vacation on my own, to England. Clare had said over the previous six months that a threesome was impossible, but I put off the decision to move out because I wanted to finish off various practical things in the house and leave it in good order.

I was coward enough to go on a business trip and called to say that I would not be coming home again. Pretty tough on my wife. I did not really think she could not have known, but she must have tried to deceive herself. We had not discussed it with the kids but they knew.

My wife remained in the house. Sadly, we met two or three times, but she could not bring herself not to attack and misjudge. The bitterness has not gone. She discovered that our son had brought his children to see me and Clare, and after that she refused to see him, or the grandchildren, and has not in fact seen them since.

Clare would have liked to have had a child. Too late. I think the divorce will be pushed through for her sake. She would like to be married. She has a semi-public job with a lot of social contacts, but she doesn't use my name.

During my life I have not sought a lot of sexual activity. I am not made that way. On the other hand, I could never go to the movies without getting a hard-on. The question of any other relationship simply does not arise now.

BRENDA

I am largely using your invitation to write as an excuse to sort out my own thoughts and ideas—never easy to do, and at last I have a constructive reason for doing so. I'm thirty-two, married at the age of twenty-four, and have a son of four and a half. I'm a college graduate with some years' teaching experience before motherhood took over, and several periods of substitute teaching since. I've also done some work in market research. My husband is also thirty-two, and a teacher. We met during our postgraduate work, and we were married some two years later.

As a teenager I think it's fair to say that my sexual experience outweighed my knowledge! I had had three encounters by the time I left school, two of them with men substantially older than me, and I was willing enough in all of these, basically because I liked them and wanted to please them. I can't say I really knew too much about what was going on at the time—sex was a taboo subject in my house. I was an only child of elderly parents and "that sort of thing" was never discussed. So despite having handled and been penetrated by three fairly substantial male organs, I went to college fairly green—the words *orgasm*, *masturbation*, and *clitoris*, for example, were completely unknown to me—and not just the words.

Inevitably I learned a lot during the next three years, and although I never "slept around," I did have some very rewarding sexual relationships and discovered that I could really enjoy sex a great deal. Again inevitably, after three years, a lot of old friendships broke up as people left the university after finals. I had chosen to stay at the same university for my teacher-training year and felt a little lost with my former boyfriends and lovers scattered around the country. I met Steve (now my husband) within the first few days of the new semester, and we were soon going out on a regular basis. Sex did not automatically follow, although I was determined that it should because I was missing it after getting plenty for certainly the last two years. But we concentrated on getting to know each other. We had very much in common, and a very loving relationship developed. When sex did come, on my initiative, it was very enjoyable. Steve was a virgin, and it made me feel good to be the more experienced one. Our sexual relationship while we were students invariably involved a "quickie" because of our domestic circumstances. Little and often seemed to be the order of the day.

Despite this relative promiscuity in my student days, when I married in 1969 I really felt that this was the one and only, and I literally hadn't wanted anyone else, in a sexual way or any other way, since becoming engaged to Steve eighteen months before—except for a brief encounter with an ex-boyfriend at a friend's wedding. The only thing that seemed to change after marriage was my attitude toward sex. To say I went right off it would be taking it too far, but instead of once or twice a day it was once or twice a week or even less. I put this down to tiredness. I had a very tiring job that involved me in a long daily trip. The responsibility of running a home was new to me—I was never very domestic—and I found it difficult to cope. I was frequently home from work with colds or the flu. We had moved to a town where the colder, damper air did not seem to suit me. Something had to go, and it was my sex life. Inevitably, Steve resented this and found it difficult to understand the change.

After three months of marriage we had a visit from an old college friend of mine. Steve had only met Jan once before as she had spent two years abroad and returned shortly after our wedding. But he had heard a lot about her from me—her zany nature and complete promiscuity figuring largely in her attributes. Despite my lack of sexual responsiveness at this time, it never occurred to me that he would try to lay her—but he did. When I discovered him in her bed in the middle of the night I went berserk. I regarded infidelity as absolutely unthinkable.

Jan left, and Steve and I patched things up, although our sex life didn't get any better, in the sense that we were having it far less frequently than before we were married—and also we seemed to be stuck in the "quickie" rut that because of circumstances we had settled in before. In fact, nearly all my sex had been like that—except with one or two boyfriends with a stronger amount of imagination or initiative than Steve—or I—possessed.

My attitude toward infidelity was as rigid as ever, although I only ever had one other occasion to get angry—which in retrospect was a very trivial and even laughable one. But at the time, the idea that a marriage partner could seek sexual stimulation elsewhere was abhorrent to me.

We moved south after two years; new jobs, house-owning for the first time, meeting new people: All took priority over improving our sex life. In every other way our relationship was still pretty good. We both have quick tempers and we fought quite often, but it was always short-lived with no grudges. Our common interests were many.

It was about this time that I became aware that I was thinking about old times at college far more and in particular two ex-boyfriends, by now both in Canada, with whom I'd had great relationships, both in and out of bed. The parents of one of them lived only thirty miles from our new house and I frequently fantasized about going to see them and making contact with Martin—but I never did anything about it. Also at this time a sixteen-year-old boy from my husband's new school developed a "crush" on me—we were working together on a charity project—and I must admit to being rather flattered by this and allowing his phone calls, visits, and occasional presents for some four or five months before deciding it was becoming a little too embarrassing. A bike accident and long stay in the hospital cooled his ardor anyway. After another year or so, the college where I was now teaching introduced a new course for which I was responsible. This brought me into contact with a number of eighteen- to nineteen-year old students, and on three separate occasions I thought "I could go for you" about those I was teaching, an attitude that would have been unthinkable in the first two years of my marriage.

I became pregnant and then miscarried at four months, which was very disturbing for both of us. We resolved to try for another baby as soon as possible—not that I am a particularly maternal type; I suppose I just wanted to prove I could do it. Consequently our sex life improved no end in the hope that I would conceive. I did. At that point I became totally wary of sex in the (mistaken, I imagine) belief that it might cause another miscarriage. We still saw Jan from time to time, although I was terrified to leave her alone with Steve in case there was a repetition of the earlier episode. In fact, during my pregnancy, the only time Steve and I had sex was when Jan was visiting. I supposed I was scared stiff of losing him to her. The rest of the time we had no sex at all. I got my sexual relief from masturbation—for the first time in my life, and all inspired by an article in *Forum* Jan had shown me. My first self-produced orgasm was fantastic—far better than anything I had achieved with Steve (he didn't know I did it)—and I suppose I got hooked on masturbation and he became very frustrated. I kept assuring him that "everything would be all right after the baby."

It wasn't, of course. I had a very difficult birth in January of 1974 and because of stitches, soreness, and psychological barriers, I didn't let Steve near me until about July. He was really frustrated, and we had some terrible arguments, fights even. I wasn't even masturbating any more, though Steve was, which I hated (irrationally), although I didn't know until much later that he was "getting some on the side" as well.

I have written all that in such detail to try to put into perspective my early and changing attitudes toward sex and marriage. That year—1974—is a turning point, for not only does it mark the birth of our son and our first real fights, but also the beginning of "the affair."

Steve taught at a local school, of course, and naturally we had a number of friends on the faculty there. One particular couple, some years older than us, we saw frequently. Bernard (Bernie, he was called) and I had always gotten along very well—we had a similar sense of humor and enjoyed exchanging quick repartee. We had a number of similar interests and were just generally friendly without making a big thing out of it.

I had always been involved in politics, and in fact this was one of the original points of contact between Steve and me, but we had opted out in 1970. In 1974 there were the local elections. I was stuck at home with a baby and felt this would be an escape from diapers and feeding. I telephoned the local party headquarters and offered to help. This spurred Steve into action—he's always regarded himself as more politically aware than me, and he disappeared out canvassing for the next couple of weeks. One evening he returned after a late session complete with Bernie, who had been engaged in a similar pursuit. After three years of knowing him, we didn't even know he was of the same political persuasion! We talked politics late into the night, and seemingly every night for the next few weeks, for after the election the two of them launched into a campaign for signing up new members and generally trying to build up the association. Their efforts were respected—Steve is a seasoned political campaigner and Bernie was a willing learner. He has a brilliant mind and borrowed book after book to absorb aspects of party history and policy. In the primary he was nominated as our candidate for the state legislature.

Inevitably during that year we saw far more of him than ever before and less of his wife, who was not interested in politics. They seemed to be going through a bad time with frequent arguments, though friends who'd known them longer said this was nothing new. As we saw more of him during the year I became increasingly attracted to him—in an intellectual sense at first, I think, but just how things evolved in my mind I'm not sure. Certainly he was always complimenting me—but then he did that to every reasonably presentable female. Nevertheless, I found it quite flattering—even though he was reputed to be "the biggest verbal adulterer in the business." Apparently he was always bragging of having had someone or other—to colleagues at work—but Steve took a lot of it with a grain of salt. We spent a lot of time together, discussing things and deepening our friendship, but he never made any suggestions about sex when we were on our own. It was always in company, mainly because it gave us both a chance to indulge in our favorite pastime of quick-fire humor, often at each other's expense.

Not a very firm basis for a relationship, perhaps, and at this time there was no "relationship," just a very close friendship. Yet I found he occupied my thoughts all the time. I was ecstatic when he visited, and totally immersed in thinking about him when he wasn't there. Politics kept us closely involved and we spent hours on the phone. Admittedly this was the first long time I'd had at home, because of the baby, so maybe I had more time to myself to think about him than if I'd been working, but by midsummer I knew that I felt about him in a way I'd never felt about Steve or any previous boyfriends. Sexual feelings were there, but they were not uppermost. I really loved that guy. I worked like crazy for a good result in the election, not so much from political commitment but from commitment to him. And I didn't say a word all this time about how I felt.

After the election, which he lost, I sat back to take stock of things and for the first time admitted that there was a strong sexual urge there. I had this feeling that he would be fantastic in bed, and I really wanted him. Things were a little better with Steve again by now, but this didn't prevent me from revolving my whole day around thoughts of Bernie. We still saw a great deal of him and I wanted him, in every way, more and more. Steve had to go away for two days once, and I was praying that Bernie would come and see me. He didn't, and I was desperately miserable, although I don't really know if I would have told him how I felt if he'd been there. I was terrified of rejection.

A few weeks later there was the school faculty dinner and dance to which Steve, I, Bernie, and Viv all went. Bernie is an excellent dancer; I am not. Being nine years younger than him I just missed the ballroom-dancing era. In previous years he had had the odd dance with me just to be polite before giving me up as a bad partner. On this occasion we spent a lot of time together, drinking and dancing, and by the end of the evening we were dancing very close together. No man has ever turned me on so much, and he was fairly aroused. I just wanted to take him away somewhere, tell him how I felt about him, and suggest we go to bed. Of course, this wasn't possible. He and Viv came to our house for coffee after the dance, and he came to talk to me in the kitchen. I sensed that he felt as I did, desperately keen but thoroughly restrained by the situation. Neither of us said anything about the way we felt, but silences said it all.

Later on, after they'd gone, Steve and I were discussing them, and Steve (never a great one for gossip) told me some things about their marriage that Bernie had told him months before. Sexually it was even less successful than our own. I had never before lost sleep over a man, but that night I did (the first of many!), I was so filled with love and longing for him.

Ironically and most frustratingly, I didn't see him for about ten days, which was an agonizing time. During that time Jan came to stay briefly, and she and I had a long talk one evening. I said that my views on marriage and fidelity had changed drastically, that I felt I was in a rut and needed some outside stimulation. I didn't specifically mention Bernie to her—mainly because she'd already met him once and hadn't liked him much, and I just couldn't bear to hear any disapproval of him at this point. Anyway, she encouraged me to be more outgoing and not just sit around waiting for things to happen. She also advocated more openness with Steve about how I felt generally.

I was able to follow her advice on the first point, but not the second. No way could I say to Steve that I was hopelessly in love with his best friend. But I called Bernie the following day and asked him if he could stop by some time. I insisted he come when Steve wasn't in, so maybe he had some idea of what was in store. In fact he came more or less immediately, that same lunchtime, which caught me by surprise as I was unprepared in what to say. Or rather I chickened out of saying: "You are the most fantastic man I have ever met in my life; I'm screaming to have an affair with you, and I'd live with you tomorrow and forever if you'd have me." Instead it came out as something very weak about not being very happy. Despite a nice house, family, etc., there seemed to be something missing.

"Well," he said, "you either need a job or a man." I pointed out that I couldn't easily get a job because the baby was too young. "Okay, a man then." "I don't know any men," I replied, right on cue. "Except for you." Point taken. We were sitting together on the couch as we often did. He put his arm around me: "Brenda, my love, come here!"

I didn't need to be asked twice. We kissed and caressed for a long time and I felt I had so much to give. My feelings were not only sexual, although I was very aroused. I remember vividly a feeling of complete happiness. When we separated he looked at me very seriously. I wanted to say, "I love you." Instead he said, "I wish I could jump in with both feet, I really do, but I am committed elsewhere and I really can't let her down." He went on to explain that he was about to apply for a legal separation from Viv because of his involvement with, of all things, a sixteen-year-old girl. I couldn't believe it. I wanted him so much, and someone else had beaten me to it. Clearly he was more than willing for a purely physical relationship with me, provided I "didn't get involved." I just couldn't bring myself to tell him how involved I was already.

He left soon after, and I was in a thoroughly confused state, not only because of the pain his revelation had caused me, but also by the mere fact of his involvement with someone else so young. He'd told me nothing about her except her name, Mary, sixteen and a half. He was thirty-eight at the time. I worried all day—more about him than about me—and this factor alone made me want to tell Steve about it, which I did about three days later—although I gave the impression that Bernie had come by to talk to me about Viv, and the break-up of the marriage, rather than saying I had invited him. I continued to fret all over Christmas, at the same time anticipating his next visit to me, because I knew that at the first opportunity we would have sex.

The opportunity came on a Tuesday afternoon in early January. He had no classes on Tuesday afternoons and that became our regular "time" for some weeks to follow, at first on my couch, and after a few weeks, with increasing confidence, I suggested we go to bed. The sex from the very beginning was everything I expected it to be. He was strong, dominating, and imaginative, and although he could only ever stay for an hour or so he made sure that we were sexually involved for most of that time. The crazy thing was that, during those early months, I never came. Orgasms have always been easily achieved for me, with every other lover, but not with Bernie. But sometimes it doesn't matter. Our bodies responded to each other so intensely that I always felt ecstatic from the experience and never let down.

Inevitably I came to resent Mary more and more, especially as I got to know more about her. I was really uptight about the situation and must have become impossible to live with. I wasn't happy unless I was with Bernie, and tried to see far more of him—more than he was prepared to accept. The more I pushed, the less he responded, and the less he responded, the more uptight I got. With the benefit of hindsight I think perhaps we should have wound it up there and then, but I was too involved emotionally and he too involved physically. Although I need continual reassurance that he means it, he says that sex with me is the best thing that has ever happened to him in bed, and that to me is very important.

It would take a book of its own for me to describe the various ups and downs in our relationship in the last three and a half years. The ups have been indescribably happy times, especially when we've been able to share a social life as well as a bed. The downs have been traumatic. I've been close to suicide twice, and only the sanity of two or three marvelous friends has kept me going.

Circumstances have changed: Steve no longer teaches at the same school, and so that point of social contact is partially lost. Bernie is no longer involved politically—I think partly because of me. He is now divorced and living on his own some forty miles away, with no telephone. Previously he was on the phone and lived ten minutes' walk away. Consequently I am now completely dependent on him to call me—which he does every two or three weeks, and we have a marvelous evening together; obviously I wish I could see him more. The changes in our physical relationship are all for the better. I still don't have an orgasm every time we have sex, but when I do it is indescribable. Our sexual technique is improving all the time, and it was pretty good to start with. Socially we see less of each other, which I desperately regret. He used to take me to the occasional party or out for a drink, and we've had a few weekends together. But now its strictly indoors only and for two or three hours at a time. Some things of course haven't changed: My love for him—and it is not just physical love—is as strong as ever.

Mary, now twenty-two, is still very much a part of his life, and so his social life involves her far more, which I resent and regret but have learned to live with. He plans to marry her, he says, and I'm sure he does, but I'm skeptical about its ever happening, although they do love each other very deeply. Theirs is not a sexual relationship and I think he's terrified of its becoming so. She knows that he and I "once had" an affair, but she thinks it's all over. Much as I can't help resenting her, there is nothing I can do—if he thought I was trying to stir things up he would leave me tomorrow, and I couldn't bear that. It nearly happened last year and I had to learn the hard way. Obviously he wishes I wasn't as involved as I am—in his more flippant moments he describes our relationship as "two friends with the same hobby—namely, screwing." At times he is more loving and says he honestly wishes that he could do the right thing for me, but he can't. "There's no future in it" is his most common expression at these times. And I must accept that. We're still together after three and a half years and there's no sign of a break-up; I suppose one day it will come, but the thought that we may always be together if something should go wrong for him is, deep down, the thing that keeps me going.

How has it affected my marriage? Well, first, Steve knows about it. I have never made any effort to publicly conceal my affection for Bernie. I found it impossible to do so, and in the days when we were all part of the same social circle Steve found this very hard to take. He has never left me, because of our four-year-old son, but he came pretty close to it once. For my part, not a week goes by without my wanting to leave. We have sex about as frequently as before, but more often than not I am completely unresponsive and bored out of my mind. When he does arouse me it's all over in five minutes and I feel let down, despite the fact that I usually come. I can only think, "It's not Bernie." He knows I have a very deep feeling for Bernie because we've discussed it. Inevitably—because he does love me, I think—it hurt him. But I can never bring myself to tell him that my sex life is a million times better once every three weeks or so when I see Bernie than it ever is with him. He and Bernie are still friends, although they see far less of each other now that they are no longer working together. They get on well still—despite the fact that Steve came home from a trip earlier than anticipated about six months ago on one of the rare evenings when Bernie was visiting me instead of vice-versa. We were in bed when Steve arrived, but we were spared the ignominy of being caught "in the act" because Steve didn't have a key and I had to get up to let him in. Steve was obviously angry and threw Bernie out, but afterwards he was more amused when he thought about how frustrated we must have felt. I think he is now pretty well resigned to the situation—in fact he suggested jokingly that I go and have a "dirty weekend with Bernard" during the school holidays because I've been very run down lately as our son has been quite ill. I'm working on the suggestion!

Other people's reactions? At first I felt that "no one must know," and yet I *wanted* people to know because I was so happy to be involved with him despite the complexities. So I dropped hints and left people to draw their own conclusions and gossip among themselves, which I'm sure they thoroughly enjoyed. It really didn't bother me who knew—because how could I be ashamed of loving someone? I always maintained that if anyone asked me about it I wouldn't deny it, but I have, twice. Once to Mary because that is imperative; and I still conceal from Steve the frequency of our meetings. I am "babysitting" or "visiting friends." It was also important to keep it from Viv before the divorce—which was very hard as she used to come to Steve and me for shoulders to cry on. Now I don't care whether she knows or not, but I never see her anymore anyway. So a lot of people know in a casual sort of way—neighbors, for example, seeing his car parked outside my house whenever Steve is away; political or school associates seeing the way we used to behave together at social functions. I don't know how these people react—if they can't accept it, that's their hang-up, not mine. The people who do matter are the very close friends that I've needed to talk to, especially when things have been going wrong. They've been very understanding and accepting of the situation—mainly because they're all having affairs themselves! As for Bernie, it's much more of a clandestine thing for him than it used to be, which may be shutting the barn door after the horse has run away. But the most important thing for him is to protect Mary. She would be so hurt if her faith in him were destroyed.

My own reactions? Clearly, it has shaken my early attitudes toward marital infidelity because nothing will stop this now—until Bernie does. I've even encouraged Steve to have brief affairs with other women because I felt that that justified my own actions a bit more. He's done that once or twice but says he isn't really interested. Do I feel guilty about it? I suppose at first I did. I kept a diary (until Steve found it), which I suppose was a way of relieving my guilt feelings. But guilt was mainly a result of the complexities with Mary that so shattered the beginnings of the relationship. Now I don't feel guilty about it at all—except about two profoundly upsetting occasions when my son has been distressed by my disturbed state, and occasions when I have refused to move from the house, waiting for the telephone to ring. This particular affair has caused me a great deal of misery and pain, but the happiness that it also brings far outweighs it. I didn't plan it. We have only one life—it's up to us to make the most of it. I feel that with Bernie I am doing that. I am giving love in a way that I can give it to no one else; I am getting friendship and a physical relationship that mean more to me than anything else life could possibly have to offer.

Both Gerald's affair with Clare and Brenda's with Bernard have interesting common features, some of which have been touched upon already, but some of which require closer examination. In both cases the two central characters found themselves resuming their personal, social, emotional, and sexual development after a period of marriage. Both went through a similar period of conventional acceptance of fidelity in marriage, and a period in which reawakened sexuality sought some new outlet. They each began progressively to love someone who was part of their social circle, and accepted by their spouse as a close friend of his or hers, and of the family unit as a whole. Neither of them acted precipitately. They moved little by little into a sexual relationship and found, once the sex started, that it had greater depths of meaning for each of them than the sex that took place in marriage. The discovery of the new partner gave a new depth of meaning to their own lives—deeper "lows," perhaps, but also greater "highs." Each faced the four main dangers as they "continued"—the problem of control, the need for secrecy, the difficulty of communication, and the problem of jealousy.

In their cases the affairs have proceeded, and spouses have been told. The angry and embittered wife of Gerald, now going through divorce, has not had an easier time than Brenda's husband, who has stayed with her for the sake of their son. Both have played family politics. Gerald's wife rejected her own child, dramatizing as the ultimate betrayal his acceptance of the new setup when he took the grandchildren to see Gerald and Clare. Steve came home to find Bernard in the house, guessed what was happening, and took perverse delight in having stopped them "in the act," thus leaving them feeling frustrated. He has left his wife feeling equally frustrated sexually many times, and perhaps it was this irony that appealed to him, that she should feel the same with her lover. The power structure of the family—in particular, that which grows up in the relationship between husband and wife—often finds a newer, clearer expression in the setting up of an affair on the one hand and reactions to its discovery on the other. The central conflict that this power structure contains, and stems from, is the inevitable separation at times of sex from love and love from sex. Neither Gerald nor Brenda says that they were primarily seeking sex, but this love for another person made more sense with sex than without it. In their marriages, love without sex made less sense, and both had ended up with sex without love. Their affairs brought both sex and love back into proportion in ways that made new sense of their lives. Attempts to do this within marriage had not only failed, but had also led to the protracted power struggles that the affairs accentuated.

Each partner—Gerald and his wife, Brenda and her husband—had to take part in a deeper form of this struggle, whether they wanted to or not, whether they liked it or not.

Each also had to face the reaction of friends and neighbors—the group of people in the community who traditionally witness marriages and whose good report rewards successful ones. The "inevitable gossip" that Gerald expected was partly forestalled when he left his wife, and he found himself surprised at how supportive his colleagues turned out to be. Brenda, by contrast, played the gossip stakes, letting people think what they might. Yet she too had friends who listened sympathetically—probably because "they were all having affairs too."

CHAPTER SIX

Why people cheat

AFFAIRS ARE USUALLY SURROUNDED by a protective web of lies and deceit. Whether an affair is a secret or not and whether it has ended or is still going on, the lies are usually designed to "protect" the marriage, or to safeguard certain aspects of the marital relationship. Many of these lies are half-truths, because the whole truth would be too painful to face up to, or might too radically alter the relationship between husband and wife.

> I did not know that he was having an affair—the family knew it but didn't tell me. My sister-in-law knew that the mistress was one of my best friends, but she was careful not to tell, even though it had gone on for a few years. . . . When they both disappeared from home, her husband, who did not realize the situation either, actually phoned to ask me where she had gone. (Sandra)

> I'm happy with my wife. I'd be horrified if she were unfaithful. For myself, I'm open to temptation. If the opportunity arose

and I knew I would not be found out, yes, I would get some on the side. I get kicks from new experiences. (Ted)

People who have affairs think deeply, very often, about why they deceive their partners. The need to justify lying is part of the general need people have to make sense of their own behavior. How people justify their excuses, half-truths, and lies is of considerable interest, both from the point of view of the particular marriage and affair in question, and generally as an insight into attitudes toward marriages and affairs. A number of justifications are found over and over again as more affairs are studied. Most of these are particularly associated with the married man or woman who is having an extra-marital affair, but some go with the role of "other woman" (or "other man"), and some with the "innocent" spouse. The "eternal triangle," as it has been called—one partner in a marriage having an affair while the other does not—calls for three dramatic roles, each of which requires its own deceits and justifications. The actors in the drama cope with guilt and fear by defending their own behavior. The form of defense they adopt can be very useful to friends, relatives, and counselors in understanding the source of guilt, the motivation for the affair, and the attitude of the people involved, both toward other participants in the drama and toward themselves.

Many of these ways in which people justify their dishonesty to people they love occur in several variations. By grouping the variations together it is possible not only to consider how people who use these justifications see their own marriages and affairs, but also to guess at the source in their childhood of some of the conflicts that are expressed through the affair. This is not, of course, an exact science. When people are is asked for advice about an affair, however professional they may be, all they can really do is listen carefully and make intelligent guesses. Yet it is as well to remember that people who deceive others, or who are deceived by others, are often deceiving themselves too, and that they probably learned to do so in ways that particularly suited them long before they were old enough to marry. To be asked for advice is common, but for people to take advice is rare, because self-deceit is so often at the root of marital conflict, and because the roots of self-deceit go so far back in childhood. Accordingly, professional counselors try not to give advice at all. That would merely reinforce self-deceit. It is much more useful to help people understand themselves their own way than to insist that they adopt a new theory about themselves from an adviser. Professional advice can encourage the sort of self-examination that can lead to people's understanding problems, if not solving them. Oliver, for example, attended a therapy group:

> She [his wife] still continued to feel a lot for me after I had stopped feeling anything much for her. She was then feeling rejected. I wanted things to go on, and I was moving more away. It was immensely distressing for her. I felt guilt about the children. I never felt I was withdrawing from them. Naturally I felt bad when things got appalling. My lover came on the scene about then. She was a friend of the working sort at first, and I became more and more fond of her, and it was impossible to allocate how much the relationship between her and me affected my marriage. I still can't sort that out.
>
> When the affair began, I started to look on home life as some sort of torture. Going home, I remember, was something I had to brace myself for. All my comfort was deposited with my lover. At some stage my wife had had a lover and in a funny sort of way she may have been doing that because she thought it was what I wanted her to do. It got her off my back a bit—no, I can't honestly say it made any difference. I was really unconsciously moving away—as if by a force I could not control.
>
> I went in for group-therapy work with my lover. All those "affairs" or "incidents" before had been quite unemotional. I began to see why they were important. I had only made love with three or four women when I married, and I suppose that there was an awareness of not knowning what more there was I had missed. I did not feel that the range of human love had been explored, and therefore I was missing out from that point of view. These incidents—the relationships—taught me a little more. I've realized that my parents' marriage was based on deep assumptions about being bound together as a couple. They assumed as much for me, that I'd be the same. Every time I met someone attractive there was a fantasy projection of life-long romance. When my wife and I split up, when I left

her, I went and lived with my parents. By that time I could not have done anything else. At that time I was forty-two.

In producing justifications for lying and deceit, the three principal actors in a marital drama—the married lover, his or her spouse, and the "other" lover—frequently give away clues as to their earliest attitudes toward sexual partnership, the attitudes they learned in childhood from their own parents and that they have transferred into adult life. The significance of the various justifications that are encountered lies in the way marital conflicts are so often a replay of childhood conflicts. By identifying a particular childhood conflict behind a marital drama, it is often possible to help the actors find new strength and understanding to cope with their problems. In the following sections, the most commonly encountered justifications are looked at in this way—first, those of the husband or wife having the affair; second, those of the "innocent" spouse; and third, those of the "other" lover.

Justifications for deceiving a wife or husband

1. "Love justifies everything."
Brenda (quoted previously) asked: "How can I be ashamed of loving someone?" Her justification for deceiving her husband is that love transforms the sordid business of deceiving him into something for which she cannot be held responsible.

Underlying this type of justification is a defense against guilt and shame about sex. It is not only the sordid business of lying but also the sordid business of sex that is transformed into something sacred and pure by the addition of love. At one extreme this attitude may be based on the myth that there is only one person in the world who will make the perfect sexual partner, and that, when this person appears, you simply fall in love and live happily ever after. Such a myth is often carefully fostered in childhood and adolescence by parents who are unsure of their own authority and sexual performance. They want their child to believe this partly because they wish to be thought of as an example of perfection themselves, and partly because they cannot bring themselves to accept the prospect of their child's experimenting sexually with many partners. If the child believes that there is only one person who is right for him or her, presumably the child will wait for the right one to come along, fall in love first, get married next, and only then have sex for the first time. The myth of the "one and only love" also occurs in the argument that the "chemistry" has to be right for a sexual partnership to work properly. Many married people who have affairs and justify them on the grounds of love say that they fell in love for the first time when they met the partner of their affair. They often give the impression that they had married without falling in love, and that they had lost faith in the myth of the one and only love, until their affair happened. They had been disappointed, almost robbed of their birthright. Now, however, they understand what it feels like to be really loved, or to be "in love," or for the "chemistry" to be right. Sometimes, when asked why they married, they will say they "thought" they were in love but were deceived, as it turned out.

Clues about guilt and shame over sex are also often present. Sexual performance is often tied to overstatements—excessive aggression, long sexual marathons, or exaggerations about how good a sexual partner the lover is compared with the spouse. The use of unlovely words for lovemaking, particularly the aggressive use of the four- and five-letter words, are also often a form of overstatement, and often indicate similarly a deep-seated fear of sex or sexual incompetence. Love transforms sex from something coarse into something beautiful, but, just as sex is often referred to in violent or exaggeratedly crude language, so, when it is transformed, the act of transformation is violent, exaggerated, and dramatic. They "fall" in love, and have the symptoms to prove it. Sex is justified by a love that will last forever. Whatever people think, the basis of such an affair is not sexual greed but pure love, and, to the pure, all things are pure.

Anthea fell in love with her young cousin. For months they kissed, fought against full physical love. Then she visited him at college.

> We slept together in the countryside. He shared an apartment with another student, the usual cramped situation. I was introduced to his roommate as his girlfriend, aged twenty-four

(I was then nearly thirty), a young secretary. *West Side Story* was showing nearby and I almost fell into the trap of saying I'd seen it ten years earlier. I was called "Ellen" for the weekend. It was terribly funny to live a lie, one of the hardest things.

The relationship was very intense and marvelous. If I die tomorrow it will be that weekend I remember. Even before that winter Saturday when we made love in the car, there was a terrific commitment. The time with him was so precious— especially with two young children at home—that when he traveled south I went with him halfway, just to be with him. We sent letters and poems through a friend, to another address, and my husband never knew until our marriage broke up.

2. "It didn't mean anything."

During an affair, the two lovers may find that although they enjoy sexual release together, they are nevertheless incompatible. This can arise in several ways. First, they may be presented with the opportunity for impulsive sexual intercourse together and embark upon an affair without expecting it to last. They may be physically unsuited, the wrong size or shape for each other, or the wrong age. Yet they carry on for a while until they discover that it does not afford much satisfaction or until something better comes along. Second, they may find that the initial attraction was solely physical, and that they are unsuited for each other by temperament. Third, they may discover that they have different tastes sexually, or had different motives for the initial sexual intercourse. When the differences emerge they accept them as irreconcilable and end the relationship.

Emotional incompatibility is less of a problem in an affair than it is in marriage. The partners are not legally bound to each other and can break up more easily than can married couples. A "trivial" or "frivolous" marriage is almost impossible. Trivial or frivolous affairs are very much more common. Nevertheless, the fact that an affair may be trivial, of no account, and certainly not a threat to marriage is seldom used to justify telling the spouse about it. Logically it might be expected that the "casual" affair of this kind would not require lies and deceit, since it is scarcely important enough to be worth protecting. What, then, lies behind this justification? A husband gave us his view on this: "Once an affair becomes known, it ceases to be a carefree outlet, and gets bogged down in the bickering and backbiting all too common when the pressures of sex become interwoven with economics and personalities, complications and prejudices." His affairs are "largely superficial and discreet," and he allows his wife to know only the type of woman he finds attractive.

The partner who has "casual" or "trivial" affairs is often part of a marriage in which sex is no longer fun. The idea of being "naughty"—of committing a few misdemeanors on the sly, and getting away with them—can be a welcome relief from the solemn act of marital-bed performance. The casual affair that does not mean anything is a kind of sexual shoplifting, not really a crime, just an act of childish delinquency. The marital partner is not informed, in the same way that a child who does something slightly wicked does not tell his or her parents. It would lead to an inquest, an embarrassing interrogation, and a reaction out of all proportion to the seriousness of the crime. Parents who overreact to such trivial forms of naughtiness are often known by their children to commit minor misdemeanors themselves. Sometimes mothers encourage their sons to be "real boys" by allowing a certain level of mischief before the line is drawn and the child is told he has gone too far. They therefore unconsciously train the young man to be a sexual delinquent, to go as far as he can without being caught. After marriage, when the husband is supposed to have settled down, the behavior re-emerges as a talent for the casual affair. To be naughty and to get away with it undetected by authority is what matters. Often, however, men have a need to boast of affairs to other men.

Sex that really matters has to do with being married, with having children, and with keeping their wife's respect, just as being a good son had to do with not letting the family down, not doing anything really bad, and not getting caught by Mother. A good son loves his mother; a good husband loves his wife. So when such a good son becomes a good husband, his sexual adventures are justified as loveless.

Married women also have affairs that "mean nothing" because they are purely sexual. The motivation for justifying deceit about affairs on the grounds that they are trivial is probably much the same for each sex. For women, the motive for the deceit is often that the man concerned was a close friend of the husband, or a former lover from carefree pre-marital history. The husband would have overreacted in much the same way as the wife of the casually delinquent husband, and would have read altogether too much into things. Wives, as much as husbands, and perhaps more so, have to suffer solemn performance in the marriage bed when they might infinitely prefer a noisy, fun, and altogether more amusing sexual encounter.

Not all affairs where the deceit is justified by the "it was meaningless" argument are naughty escapades replaying a childhood act of delinquency. Sometimes marital infidelity is an expression of deliberately meaningless sex designed not to be enjoyed. For some people sex is not fun, and never has been. For others it may have been fun once, but because of doubts about their own self-confidence, or the fits of depression that can come as a result of crises, sex becomes simply a way of obtaining a temporary end to deep loneliness and bitter thoughts of self-rejection. A sex act undertaken casually with a stranger can then be meaningless in the sense that there was no mutuality in it. Such casual affairs are designed, perversely, to underline the self-rejection the person already feels. They may persist, as devoid of meaning as when they began. All they offer is the presence of another human being, and some small consolation in the pretense that he or she cares. When the pretense ends, the affair often ends too, and nothing is said about it because nothing could have been said about the loneliness that invaded the marriage. This tendency is reminiscent of the neglected child whose parents set no limits because they never saw the need to care either way. The parallel crime is not that of shoplifting but rather that of stealing from the parents. Repeated, meaningless, casual affairs that never work sexually are a cry for help, a despairing self-rejection, proving and re-proving that nobody loves the person concerned, and that nobody can love him or her. The fantasy underneath is that the person concerned is too evil to be loved, an orphan whom nobody wants.

"It didn't mean anything" can also be a lie. To justify the deceit and the fear that arise from a deeply important affair, one that might under other circumstances have been the gateway to a different kind of life, people sometimes tell themselves that the affair meant nothing after all. What they really mean is that the affair did not come to anything, although it might have, and nearly did. There is often an element of self-sacrifice in this. If so, there will probably be other clues indicating a need for sacrificial offerings—as an adult to placate a bad conscience, but in childhood to appease a morally indignant parent. The marriage may have been a financial struggle at the start, as many are, but in these cases the details will be recalled vividly. The parents probably expected gratitude and made sacrifices themselves so that their child would be a success in life and owe them gratitude and submission in return. Not to tell, to deceive on the grounds that an important affair was really unimportant, is to nurse a grievance or to savor the pain of what might have been but never was. The marriage may well be a union between two people who suffer in silence. They stay together for the sake of their children and—like their parents before them—expect at least a little gratitude.

3. "It had nothing to do with my wife/husband."

The basic commitment of marriage is to a joint emotional development through loving each other exclusively. It is impossible, however, to separate emotional and sexual development from intellectual growth; and for some married people their own growth can result in their feeling that they have outgrown their partner, and that they need new stimulation to meet their need to go on growing. "My wife/husband doesn't understand me" is accepted by most people as no more than a cliché on which to base a lustful affair. In fact it is frequently a revealing statement about a marriage. It can indicate that the partners have now diverged in their personal growth to the point where frustration will turn into breakdown if new sources of stimulation are not found. The marriage may appear to be placid and fulfilling on the surface, but underneath it is hollow. The two people who undertook that commitment are already living separate lives and feel unable to share with each other the important events in their private development, only those in their "public" development—the decisions about children, finances, social activities, housing, and career. Typically, "my wife doesn't understand me" is the standard line of the busy executive to his secretary, and stems from his earlier commitment to the intellectual and social development of his personality through his work. While his wife is left at home, her brain starved of exercise, he is faced daily with challenges that stretch him and that, increasingly, she cannot share. Eventually she finds him intolerant and impatient, feels and becomes less attractive, and he finds her trivial and incapable of equal partnership in the matters that concern him most. Both husband and wife in this situation may find that they have drifted apart, and each suspects that the other secretly (or openly) despises the other. The uncompleted agenda of childhood and adolescence—the parts of their personality, the interests and ambitions that are unfulfilled—may now assume a new importance. As these are private matters, to do with the individual alone, and as the circumstances prevent easy sharing, it becomes simpler to start again with someone else, to begin an affair in which separate development is less lonely, more rewarding than it would be in the marriage. Yet the official marriage is often undisturbed.

Alice's love for her husband was dying, but she had experienced no contrast to him that would have enabled her to find out what she was missing, until a legislative candidate for whom she was canvassing invited her to lunch.

> I knew that he would want to sleep with me, but I still went. I took a small bottle of brandy. I thought it might relax me. I went to the bathroom after lunch and had a good swig from it. He had given indications. "You don't have to rush off, do you?" We drove around the park. I felt complete fear, not sexual attraction. Something made me feel that I had to do this. He is twelve years older, has four children, and is married, and had an incredible history of infidelity. I did not know why, but I had to find out from someone experienced. He kissed me a lot, he tried to go further, but I said I couldn't. He found me so exciting, he said, that he had an orgasm just kissing me. I believed him. He asked me to lunch again. He rushed through it, and took me to a sleazy hotel where he booked a room. Obviously he was known there. He knew the routine. "Send up coffee immediately." I was trembling with fright. Nothing was said. The minute I had had my coffee I started to take my clothes off. There was something so blatant in his approach— I think it was probably a turn-on. I was not looking for an emotional involvement—just a purely sexual meeting.

She returned home, not intending to disturb the marriage.

Why it can in so many similar cases go on undisturbed is often because the people concerned have a facility for detachment, for separating their lives into different compartments, and for not allowing one set of feelings and activities to interfere with the others. One part of them is used in the marriage; another part is used in the affair. It is a kind of marital "moonlighting," not dissimilar to that of those people who work at two jobs and never let their loyalty to one employer interfere with their loyalty to the other. To conduct affairs of this kind without being defeated by conflicting loyalties requires a great deal of skill, and this may be part of its appeal. The narrow escapes, the emotional balancing acts, the feeling of tension, of being face to face with disaster, are not unlike those experiences that are applauded when faced successfully by mountaineers or singlehanded yachtsmen. A placid and success-ful marriage can be boring. To jeopardize it can be to feel the thrill once more of facing danger. So the lies and deceit become a means of feeling alive in a more valuable way, of doing something with a part of the self that the marriage no longer uses and perhaps never did. The problem, of course, is that the affair may well become more significant than the marriage in such an absolute way that detach-ment is shattered, and the marriage with it. The husband or wife may not have understood the person who had the affair; equally the lover may not understand why the marriage persists, and why he or she has to accept the role of prop to a partnership that fundamentally does not work as well as the secret liaison does. Ironically, in the interview quoted above it was Alice's experienced lover who lost his composure—he never intended his involvement to interfere with the rest of his life, but, as Alice described the outcome:

> He fell into his own trap. No one could have been more surprised than he. He kept saying, "I've never fallen before." I suddenly left my husband, and eventually we moved in together. Before that he was so jealous, and so worried about leaving his wife, that he paid men to make a pass at me and invite me out. He paid them to invite me to a theater and dinner and give him the honest truth about my reactions.

In the end all the partners in this affair had to become more involved as his detachment crumbled.

The childhood equivalent of "It has nothing to do with him/

her" is probably the situation in which the child holds together the marriage of its parents, the mother who would have left "if it weren't for you," and the father who effectively splits the child's loyalties in response. By choosing the right side in each quarrel, the child learns to be committed to neither, but rather to hold the balance of power and manipulate the situation to his or her own advantage. Different behavior is produced to suit the differences between the parents. This early grounding in the politics of family life may be excellent training for a later career in the politics of business, personnel management, and other positions of power. Sex, too, is often a means of power for such people, just as it was the subtle use of the child's sexuality in the family that assuaged the wrath of the parents toward each other. The need to feel attractive, and to prove that the attraction still works, is often important to them and shows in the way they dress and in their general nonverbal behavior. Such people are attractive, and know it.

4. "He doesn't tell me about his; so why should I tell about mine?"

The competitive "tit-for-tat" affair, in which a married person gives the impression that the marriage is a race to score the most extra-marital points, is probably the cruelest of marital games, since it is designed to use the lover as a pawn in the power struggle between married partners. It is not to be confused with the "open marriage," where there are agreed rules about who tells what. Some people may be sophisticated enough to feel detached about sex in this way and to see fidelity in different terms.

So-called "open" marriages are merely disguised games of tit-for-tat. In cases where not telling is justified on the grounds that the other partner has affairs that are not revealed, and where the lies and the deceit are built on the assumption that each partner in the marriage is having affairs, there is often no real proof that this is so. An assumption that is never challenged or tested is not a valid one. The "understanding" may not exist at all. Indeed, the implication is that the marriage is so built upon lies that another set will not do any more damage than what has already been done. So this could be a lie also.

What is going on in such a marriage? It resembles a succession of temper tantrums, a kind of pie fight in which people throw grenades instead of cream pies, where the object of the exercise is to hurt each other more than one was hurt the last time. The competition is to be the hurt child, to come off best in the rejection stakes. Each one wants the last word. Each is happiest when most miserable. The equivalent childhood behavior arises when a parent always rewards the tantrum by giving more attention to it than to more reasonable behavior, when violence and force are seen in the home to be the most potent means of gaining approval or getting one's own way. Sarcasm, which belittles an honest attempt to achieve something, and forces a child to pretend to succeed and to cover up failure, is often an important factor in the home as well. The child learns to fail in order to get attention, and is ignored unless the required amount of failure is produced. If two such children grow up and marry each other, escaping from home backgrounds where they cannot win into a new one where each might win, they can become competitors in failure, rewarding each other with the sado-masochistic tool of sarcasm. The irony is that they matter far more to each other than to their extra-marital lovers, or to their children, who will probably "escape" into similar marriages at the earliest opportunity.

5. "I make it right in other ways."
The idea that a marriage depends on the happiness of the individual partners, and that how they achieve this is of less importance than its effects, lies behind this group of attitudes to justify deceit. In principle it is "What he/she doesn't know cannot hurt him/her" combined with "If I were unhappy it would be far worse." So the purpose of the affair is to extend the life of the marriage, to keep one partner happy by means that are kept secret so that the other partner benefits. In this way the lies can be seen as "white lies," designed to keep everyone happy. The married person having the affair is seen as passing on the benefits of being loved illicitly through the legitimate relationship of marriage. Provided his or her lover accepts this role, affairs of this kind can have a rock-like stability, and become parallel or quasi-bigamous marriages. The guilt is adequately assuaged by careful and, as far as possible, equal attention and love from the person having the affair to both spouse and lover. Often, in cases of this kind, lover and spouse are socially connected, as friends, neighbors, or colleagues. The lover has the

major disadvantage, in that he or she carries the burden of jealousy to save the spouse from feeling it, and to avoid upsetting the carefully constructed balance of power. This is frequently offset by a feeling of deep love for both married partners, and sometimes for their children, and by the belief that he or she has fewer ties and is really free to go.

The person who comes off best in this situation is the married person having the affair, in the classic "best of both worlds" position. To be loved by two people figures in many normal fantasies, since it is the child's greatest ambition to possess both parents equally and to be the center of both their lives. But there has to be a double standard. The parents are both there in order to put the child first, so if either one loves somebody else as well as the child, its position as the center of the universe is instantly threatened. Just as the parents are not allowed to love two people equally—they can *pretend* to love each other, of course, as much as each loves the child—so the adult having an affair of this kind is shocked and horrified if his spouse or lover takes another lover. Both his or her lovers—the legitimate one and the illicit one—are jealous and possessive loves. Because the lies on which such a system is based are seen as white lies, and the infidelity is seen as an extension of true fidelity, if either of the two loved ones tries to do the same thing and set up a similar system for themselves, this is interpreted as gross disloyalty and cruel betrayal.

Alice had moved into an apartment with her lover. While she was away on a business trip, he said he would see if his wife would take him back for a week. He figured that both women wanted him and he told Alice that she had his permission to have sex with another partner. This conversation took place on the way to the airport, and by the time she arrived in Rome for the fashion shows she was feeling insecure.

> I allowed myself to be picked up by a handsome Italian, and we went out to dinner, danced, and returned to the hotel where we spent the night together. The next day Bob [her lover] arrived unexpectedly. I told him what had happened. He was demented—more so even than when he lost his father. He was so demented that the subject was brought up every

day for eighteen months. Now he says that that was what started him having other women. He felt so cheated. I later discovered that he had been sleeping with other girls all along.

It had such an appalling effect that I did not sleep with anyone else. I loved him madly, as a father figure, but I had reservations about his other women. For six years I could not accept that he was having them. I only realized it when we moved next door to his mistress.

Less-significant affairs—the ones that are said to be meaning-less because they were only sex and not love—are also justified in this way sometimes. An affair may be the proving ground for new sexual experiments that are then used in the marriage. The question, "Wherever did you learn to do that?" can now be met with the answer, "I read about it in a book." Or the affair may provide a degree of emotional or sexual reassurance from which the marriage in turn derives real benefit. "Making things right in other ways," by being kinder or more gentle with the wife or husband, is often one of the good results of secret affairs, acceptable to the spouse as a spontaneous act, but quite unacceptable if seen as the result of infidelity.

6. "He/she just couldn't take it."

To tell about an affair, or to have the "faithful" partner discover it, is often the one crisis that is hardest of all to face in marriage. Many people justify the deceit on these grounds alone: that it would destroy at one blow all the trust and faith in each other on which the marriage is based. After that, it is assumed, there would be endless doubt and suspicion, jealousy and pain forever more. The sad fact is that many marriages are based on a disproportionate degree of emotional dependence by one partner on the other. Often the admission of infidelity does destroy trust, and the marriage is never the same again. It is understandable if the risk of telling and the pain this might bring seem to be too great to face. Yet this is not always so. Telling can change a marriage for the better, by helping partners adjust to each other at a more realistic level, enabling them to undertake a new and deeper commitment to each other. Never-theless it is risky, and it is impossible to predict the possible range of reactions.

The principle of not telling in order to avoid inflicting pain is, in many cases, a cover for not telling in order to avoid facing up to responsibility. The person who does not tell and excuses the deceit or half-truths in this way is not merely protecting the partner but also protecting him- or herself. It is a patronizing position to be in, since it assumes that the partner would not be mature enough to face the facts. But it is also self-indulgent, since it gives the unfaithful partner an excuse not to face them either. One may be deceived, but the other is just as likely to be self-deceiving. By keeping the guilt a secret, the guilty person can also be self-punishing, covering up and not facing the true reason for the affair, which is often a need to have a guilty secret, and to feel bad about it.

A very confident, poised husband told us: "We have discussed infidelity, and I have convinced her that I am faithful, except for the odd nagging suspicion. I tried to foster her confidence—it makes life easier. I do basically love her and would not willingly, or rather knowingly, hurt her."

Another husband who met a girl at a disco explained away a night out. "I said I got drunk. I had to say something because I did not go back until the morning. She asked me more, but I stuck to the truth with a few omissions. I think it would have hurt her if she knew—probably a sense of betrayal. I guess she was asleep and did not worry."

"It would be too painful" very often means "I would be too painful." "It would shatter our marriage" means "I would shatter our marriage." The equivalent childhood position is to have been so badly behaved as to be beyond forgiveness, to have provoked such parental wrath that the child is not worth forgiving. For the guilty party to say that the spouse is not mature enough to accept the facts and not responsible enough to eventually react in a wise manner is not merely to fear the total loss of love that might result but also to project onto the spouse the full force of a rejection that the guilty person has already achieved singlehandedly. In some marriages one partner may have deep misgivings about his or her own capacity for self-rejection, and, having achieved a partial adjustment to this, may appear the stronger partner, the one on whom the other leans. Their courtship and marriage may have occurred during the period of adjustment, so that the self-rejecting partner chose another, worse self-rejector. Their dependency would provide reassurance at first. As the marriage develops, the adjust-ment to self-rejection may accelerate but then slow down. Now, instead of needing someone to protect, the person needs a prop for himself and finds this through an affair. The marriage has to be protected from this, because the weaker partner is now so dependent that he or she would panic if the apparently stronger partner revealed his or her weakness.

The fear of never being forgiven for something is present in many people's lives as part of the normal response to many of the major forms of child control used by parents in our culture. In childhood the fear is seldom justified: Parents usually forgive in the end. Nevertheless, there is often a very high price for being forgiven, and the period of anger that leads up to forgiveness is often designed by parents to create the maximum degree of fear. Parental rejection— temporary though it is—is the commonest form of discipline. To young children with no sense of time, it can seem permanent and be utterly terrifying, as indeed it is meant to seem. Many adults, brought up in this way, and motivated by the fear of permanent rejection and the final breakdown of marriage, play for time by deceiving their partners as to how far apart they have really become. When an affair becomes more important than the marriage, and a decision has been made to end the marriage in favor of the affair, there is often a great deal of hesitation and delay. Choosing the right moment is virtually impossible: There is no right moment. Yet people try to find it, put it off, worry about it again, agonize over it. Like the child who has been told he will never be forgiven, and cannot in his terror take a temporary rejection as anything but permanent, the sense of time is lost, and the moment of reckoning seems like an eternal nightmare.

Attitudes of the spouse

If the unfaithful husband or wife represents the first corner of the "eternal triangle," the non-offending spouse represents the second corner. It is usually he or she who is being unwittingly defended by the tissue of deception that surrounds the affair. If the cover-up works effectively, and no affair is suspected, it could be argued that such people are entirely blameless, and never find themselves called upon to justify deceit in marriage. Yet there can be very few married people who have never thought about the possibility that their partner might have or be having an affair at some time during a marriage. Most people develop attitudes toward their partner's infidelity. Often they discuss the issue, either in relation to acquaintances known to be having affairs, or in terms of their own attitudes to their particular partners. The partners who have secret affairs usually also have a clear idea of the attitude of their spouse, and many are careful to check frequently during the course of an affair to see whether attitudes have changed or hardened. So the person in the second corner of the triangle is often contributing to the deceit, determining by his or her attitude how far he or she is deceived, sometimes conniving at it, often pretending it could not happen while knowing that it is. Because the affair and its deceit are so often grown-up versions of childhood power crises, the "innocent" spouse's attitude stands in lieu of the parents' attitude learned in childhood. In the following section, some of the most commonly encountered attitudes are listed and discussed.

1. "I'd rather not know."

This attitude can be presented in a number of ways. One of these is: "Don't ever come and tell me you're having an affair." Another is: "Don't think I'd forgive you if you ever told me." The emphasis is upon telling, and, just as a child responds to the injunction "Don't tell me you've done such-and-such" by doing it and not telling, so the spouse gets the message that the faithful partner would be hurt most by news of the deed and less by the deed without the news. The implication is that the spouse (or child) can do anything he or she likes and can get away with it, provided it is not serious enough to warrant confession. It is, of course, an open invitation to deceit. What is more serious is that, by encouraging a lack of communication about minor infidelities, one is asking to be told only about the serious ones, and of these there is precious little forewarning. "I'd rather not know until I have to know" means that by then it may be too late to save the marriage.

In many cases, "I'd rather not know" goes deeper, because it also means that the married person would rather not know all about his or her partner's sex drive and sexual needs. Where their needs are very much at variance (and this is usually due to failure to spot the problem when it arises and then to work at it together) one partner may well opt out sexually, failing to respond spontaneously to the other's advances, and tacitly encouraging a search for sexual satisfaction elsewhere. Many virgin marriages—the kind hallowed by the traditional morality—encounter this problem early, and the more libidinous spouse goes off to gain the new experiences that marriage was supposed to have prevented. When Carla was twenty-one she married a man of twenty-three. She was a virgin and he had had one other girl. "Marriage was all right. On the other hand I was frightened of sex at that stage, and did not really enjoy it with him. He was so tired afterwards, and said I was insatiable. I thought there must be more to enjoy."

Another woman who married young had a similar reaction (in both cases after the first child was born). "I wanted to find out what sex was about. I was sure that sleeping with one man was not everything. I was still sleeping with my husband, but it was more exciting when I took a lover. My husband had made it quite clear he would not want to know and he seemed pleased with the result."

Often both partners have then settled for a sad deprivation—the one who goes off to find new, illicit partners never learns the techniques of deep and mature sexual love and tenderness, but repeats the cycle of exploratory sex; and the one who stays faithful is confirmed in the disillusion that provoked the early rejections. "I'd rather not know" becomes a barrier to communication—not just verbally, but sexually, too.

2. "It can't be much fun."

This line of argument suggests that all affairs must be sleazy, sordid gropes, in which the partner who tells lies in order to snatch a few hours with his or her lover in the car is more to be pitied than to be blamed. At one level it is permissive, but at another dismissive—a version of the injunction often given to teenagers to "do what you like as long as you don't enjoy it." In the teenage injunction, of course, the advice not to enjoy it is implied rather than spoken, and, as an attitude of faithful spouses to potentially unfaithful partners, "It can't be much fun" really means "Don't ever let it be more fun than it is with me." In many marriages this is probably a tall order, but then only a fairly confident spouse would risk this attitude.

At a deeper level, however, "It can't be much fun" can mean "*I* can't be much fun." Husbands and wives who take this view may be unconsciously admitting that they are less fun than they used to be. They run the risk of producing the excuse on the part of their marital companion that an affair will not be robbing them of anything they would appreciate. If the admission is not unconscious, but a truthful assessment of reality, it can, however, represent the instruction "Go ahead and have some fun; you deserve it." This may not be uncommon in a good, mature marriage, and it can bind a deeper friendship between the partners, provided the affairs are just fun, and do not lead to a deep emotional attachment that supplants the marriage.

George, a devoted husband who has balanced his affairs with his marriage, said:

> It would be okay for my wife to have affairs, so long as she had few enough not to reach beyond my level. I feel that I could betray her if I found someone with whom I established an emotional *and* physical link. But because I had a vasectomy I would not betray in the one sense that she might—the possibility of her getting pregnant is a great danger. Suddenly I would be dragged into an entirely different situation.

3. "I'd scratch her eyes out."

This is essentially the archetypal female response. The attitude is interesting in that the anger is directed not so much against the erring partner as against the lover. The forgiving of the partner is assumed, presumably after a suitable period in purgatory. Perhaps part of the assumption is that the "other woman" is always to blame. A wife described the mistress: "She was like me, small, blonde, neat, but just a bit flirty, and my mother, who suspected her motives, said, 'Watch her.' " She is seen as a rival, the bitch, the scarlet-painted whore who gives it away for nothing, the cheap floozy who seduces her husband, the thief who can't come along and ask nicely but has to go sneaking around stealing other people's men. She has two horns and a forked tail. Slow torture would be too good for her. The underlying attitude toward the husband is that he is, and always has been, weak, unreliable, and easily tempted. He is placed in the role of the naughty boy led astray, who can be dealt with by a good smack and a withdrawal of privileges for a while. Essentially he is seen as wanting to be forgiven, whether he actually does or not.

Tom, who admits that he "can't resist a woman who attracts," had to appeal to his wife recently when he was suspended for having had an affair with a colleague.

> I suppose this situation could have happened before. My wife reacted pretty well, and for a while my marriage was stronger. This enabled me to discuss things in detail with my wife and we talked of parting, saying that on such and such a date we would come to a decision, but when the date came it passed as though it meant nothing. When my wife says, "Let's work the relationship out," five minutes later, she is talking of years ahead, plans for us together. My wife's not a bad person, but I'm not quite happy with her and it's not her fault. She's a good cook and still fun in bed—I still enjoy sex with her, but that's not difficult. Even last weekend I felt I was missing out— there's no one particular at the moment. So I stayed in and watched television. I'm not even sure what I want; I still have feelings for my wife, and in the short run I can't justify what I do. Maybe I've got something women want—one girl traveled two hours just to see me for an hour on several occasions. The children don't know—it's never mattered to them, but they may have felt I was neglecting them at times. My wife simply does not ask.

This attitude of wanting to be forgiven partly flatters and partly demeans the man. It seems to be related to the child-rearing system referred to earlier, whereby the little boy who is much loved is often encouraged to be mischievous. If it is a less-common attitude toward infidelity among men, this is probably why. Girls are not encouraged to be naughty in the same way, and sexual aggressiveness and adventurism are far less likely to be condoned in wives than in husbands.

4. "A wife always knows."
This is pure myth. Almost certainly most wives never know, and a good many never even suspect. One actually learned to play racquetball to be able to play the game with her husband. But his

"racquetball lessons" were spent off the court. As an attitude toward marital infidelity, this myth is a clear challenge to those husbands who feel the need for an adventure or two to go ahead and never be caught. It implies that, since she always knows, that will stop the matter there and then. It also implies that she need never be told, and, at a deeper level, that real communication in the marriage is unnecessary because accurate and dependable telepathy already exists. Mind reading is in fact a very poor substitute for talk, and dependence on it implies an inability to care enough about someone to take the trouble to discuss problems. The equivalent child-control system, of course, is "Mother can always tell," she can "see by your face that you've been up to something." In marriage, presumably, she believes that her husband will be so weakened by any extra-marital exertions as to be unable to meet her own demands.

5. *"He'll always come back to me."*
This is the attitude of tenacious optimism, on a par with "I'll always be his mother," but less likely to be true. At its best, this approach is a form of trusting and loving, and those wives who can say it truthfully and with confidence have achieved a deep attachment in their marriage, equivalent to the bonding of mother and son. At its worst, the optimism can be founded on nothing more substantial than the myth of the only true lover, the Prince Charming who alone is right for Cinderella, the romantic hero whose love is written in the stars and cannot be unwritten. Somewhere between the best and the worst stand most wives, believing that their husbands ultimately will not stop loving them, and will not desert them, if only because all the good times and the shared triumph over bad times will bind them together forever.

6. *"It's a chance you've got to take."*
This is the attitude of straightforward realism. The chances of infidelity in each marriage are high. To spend most of the time worrying about it in case it might happen would be to never have a moment's peace. But the expression of this attitude cuts both ways. The husband or wife who says these words is also implying, *"I'm* a chance you've got to take." The risk of infidelity is not confined to the one partner. If infidelity were to be discovered, the response would almost certainly include a tit-for-tat affair.

Many married couples, however, firmly reject this view. If

marriage means anything, they argue, it means that you no longer take this particular chance. To admit that the chance is there at all is to risk encouraging it. Nevertheless, the threat by a wife that if her husband has an affair, so will she, can be an effective sanction in some cases. The double standard that men may and women must not have affairs is still very much alive, and men are often far more shocked by their wife's affairs than wives are by those of their husbands. In the final analysis the double standard can be justified only by blatantly sexist arguments, and one contemporary change of importance is that men increasingly see the weakness of such arguments.

7. Connivance.

One form of connivance has already been mentioned, the "I'm not much fun, go and enjoy yourself; you deserve it" argument. There are a great many more forms of connivance: those spoken openly, those hinted at, and a few unconscious ones. One group is ironical, and it occurs when the spouse is having a "secret" affair that has been discovered, and the other spouse has good reason to encourage it, without letting out the fact that it is no longer a secret. This can happen when both are having affairs, but it can also happen when the "innocent" partner has already withdrawn from the marriage in all but the most formal ways. "I hope she gets more out of him than I do!" is one such version. The idea is not to make life any easier for the cheating husband, but to make him pay much more effectively than if she admitted that she knew. Connivance of this kind is pure power struggle, and it is related to the tit-for-tat marital game wherein both partners compete at making themselves and others miserable. Often, when a marriage is dead but not yet ended formally, a spouse will connive with the other lover to get the married partner to accept the fact. Other forms of connivance occur when a spouse who wishes to accept a sexual withdrawal, or who wants to start an affair too, pushes the other spouse into situations where affairs are most likely. This, on the face of it, can be for the kindest reasons, motivated by pure altruism. Underneath, however, the objective is to be the victor in virtue, so that the conniving partner's guilt about a subsequent affair is assuaged on the grounds that this was simply a reaction to the manipulated partner's prior infidelity.

The "other person"

Then there is the third corner of the triangle, the "other woman" or the "other man." In the traditional version of the eternal triangle he or she is unmarried and unfettered. In fact, he or she is probably just as likely to be married, and to someone who is also having an affair with someone else who is also married. The triangles multiply, but the roles in the drama are essentially the same. In this section, the attitudes of the "other woman" in justifying the deceit necessary to keep an affair going are examined. Because those "other women" who are married really belong in the "married" category dealt with in the first section of this chapter, we have concentrated on attitudes associated with unmarried women having affairs with married men. As for the "other man," unmarried and having affairs with married women, he will be looked at later.

1. "I try not to let it worry me."

The "other woman" in the eternal triangle, particularly if she loves her man and is involved in a long-term affair, is likely to hear a great deal about her lover's wife and what goes on in his marriage. She often has the choice of getting to know the wife, and deciding for herself how she fits into the marriage. Many become, or start off as, friends of the whole family, knowing the children, joining family parties and even holidays, and developing a close relationship with the "wronged" wife. Under these circumstances she can find herself living on a knife-edge of jealousy, and must at all costs avoid letting her feelings for the shared man show. She knows many things also to which she cannot refer, and she may well make an occasional slip, particularly if she has not checked first with the man to see what he has told his wife. The deceit is very often more a matter of half-truths than downright lies, a smokescreen designed to prevent situations in which real lies and outright denials will become necessary. Should the wife accidentally or by design ask her a direct question about her feelings toward the man, or should she ask if an affair is going on, she must be ready with her answer, not too pat, but acted out as though she had never expected the question.

Under these circumstances many mistresses simply try not to let the lying worry them. It is part of the price they pay to have their share of the man. Most long-term lovers would rather have the whole man, and hope to achieve this some day. In the meantime they stay as lovers because they appreciate the difficulties and share them with the man. So for many extra-marital "wives," the deceit is seen as a short-term strategy, justified as long as it does not last too long, and as long as it saves their man from the sort of crisis that might lead him to reject her and choose the marriage instead. If she eventually wins her man and becomes his next official wife, the lies will have been justified, and she need never see the ex-wife again. Her man, however, will have to carry the major burden of guilt, since, particularly if he has children, he may continue seeing the former wife for some time after the divorce and remarriage.

Not all mistresses are sure that they want the marriage to end. One reason may be that they feel uncertain about the responsibilities, particularly many of the menial tasks that wives usually undertake, and about what some husbands may be rather finicky—the washing and ironing of shirts and handkerchiefs, for example. In situations where the man expects the wife to be his housekeeper, while a woman remains a mistress and not wife she can avoid this role and leave it to the wife. Often in such cases there are contrasts between the well-run, orderly wife and the chaotic, anarchic other woman: The shared man may enjoy the change, as long as his shirts are still available on the basis he is accustomed to expect from his wife; but if he gives up the well-run home for the chaotic one, he may well start to attempt to turn the anarchic mistress into an orderly wife. So if she is uncertain about whether she really wants her man as her husband—for whatever reason—the mistress will be more likely to use the lies and the deceit with great care, avoiding the precipitation of a crisis. Some mistresses, on the other hand, are perfectly clear about what they want, and go all out to get it. The lies are kept to a minimum in order to force the man to choose. Each refusal to lie, each hesitation in backing up the man's deceit, puts pressure on him to make up his mind and leave the wife. By saying that the lies are more of a problem for the husband, a mistress may be indicating that she is running out of patience and starting to force her man into a crisis and a decision about the marriage.

2. "It doesn't bother me at all."
Just as the wronged wife, when she finds out about her husband's infidelity, may see the "other woman" as an evil witch, so the

unmarried mistress of a married man may also characterize his wife as a hateful person who inflicts such misery on her man that all she wishes to do is get him away and kiss him better. This is to some extent the "love justifies everything" attitude, and maternal as well as romantic love are often combined powerfully. It is easier to sustain if the two never meet, and since sometimes this attitude is fostered by the husband quite deliberately and with intent to deceive the mistress, often makes sure that they do not meet.

At a less extreme level, some mistresses take the view that, if the wife were a "real" wife, the affair would not have happened anyway. The wife need not be seen as a monster, merely as less of a woman than the mistress. She deserves the lies as a punishment for failure rather than for evil. She has failed, and the mistress has succeeded, and there the matter ends: She can think what she likes. She deserves the lies.

3. "Being a mistress is more honest than being a wife."

Some women refuse to play the role of "other woman" because they have equally rejected the role of wife. To them the prospect of enforced monogamy is abhorrent, and the idea of a special status derived from an hour or so in church, synagogue, or judge's chambers and a ring on the correct finger is quite ridiculous. Sex may be for fun sometimes, and at other times for the deep, mature, shared pleasure of two loving adults in total harmony. Whether the man is married or not is irrelevant—he is a person, and as capable or incapable of loving and sharing as any other person. Their attitude is neither to justify deceit nor to reject it in favor of honesty at any price. They take the decisions about lying not on principle but on whether they seem likely to work at the time or not. In their view, marriage fosters hypocrisy. All the pomp and ceremony that surround it are a sham. Leave people alone to do what they think is best, they argue, and marriage, with all its hollow posturing, will be unnecessary. Marriage inevitably traps people into dishonesties, and makes it more, not less, difficult to live an honest life.

For the unmarried woman, particularly if she has no children, this is an extremely difficult stand to take. She has to work against a lifetime of social conditioning by a society that is above all a marrying society. Marriage and children are seen as inseparable, so that if she wants children she is taught that she must be married first, and if she is married that she has to want to have babies. All her life she will have found people only too willing to tell her that she is not really a woman until she is a wife, and that even then she cannot be a real wife unless she is a mother too. To reject both, solely on the grounds of rational argument, requires intellectual courage of a high order. Moreover, a woman who rejects either marriage or having children may have grounds other than those expressed in any rationalization she may voice.

For some unmarried mistresses of married men, the attitude that comes out as a reasoned rejection of marriage seems to be a rationalization of despair at ever being married. The marriage of her own parents may have disillusioned her about marriage in general, particularly if she lived daily with gross hypocrisy at the time in her adolescence when truth and idealism seemed of paramount importance. Her sex life with an experienced and mature man may seem so rich and full compared with the fumblings of her peers that she infinitely prefers it, despite all the difficulties of seeing so little of him when she needs him most. She may be more career-minded, more ambitious, than many of her contemporaries, and not wish to jeopardize her chances of work achievements for marriage, where she may be trapped into having children and becoming a housewife. Or she may feel that no one will marry her, either because she is unsuitable, or because the marrying kind of men will never be her kind too.

For others, the emotional reasons for rejecting marriage stem not from the idea of being a wife but from unwillingness, fear, or even revulsion at the idea of being a mother. Other women's babies may be attractive enough, but she would not feel competent to cope full-time with one of her own. Feeding, changing, bathing a baby, being tied down to a house and a routine may seem not only tedious but altogether too much to face. Actually going through with the messy, undignified, and painful process of birth may seem a revolting idea. Such feelings are not solely the province of the unmarried woman; many married women share them. The psychology that lies behind such attitudes is sometimes complex, and too readily dismissed as trivial nonsense, or labeled as deep psychosexual neurosis. But for the person caught between a need for a regular, satisfying sex life and the bonds of broodiness that often go with it on the one hand, and aversion at the thought of having babies on the other, rejection of the whole idea of marriage may be more than a simple convenient excuse, and less than a symptom of emotional break-down. By choosing as a lover a man who is already married, such a woman can give herself time to think about the question, help in sorting it out if it is a problem, sexual peace and satisfaction while she does so, and reassurance that she is attractive enough to find a husband should her feelings change.

Some do not reject the idea of marriage and motherhood, but do not feel ready yet. They enjoy being single, and their "honesty" is an overstatement in reaction to heavily emphasized attempts by parents to get them marriage-minded in adolescence. Some parents believe that finding a man is a matter of strategy, of playing him along, of telling the right white lies, trotting out the correct bits of flattery. This may be what they did, either because they are calcu-lating, or because when men were in short supply and so many women finished up "on the shelf," they had little choice. Their daughters are unlikely to feel the same pressure today, since there are more men to choose from, because there is less ignorance about sex, and because contraceptives are more widely used. To marry before you are ready simply because you have reached a certain age seems nonsensical to them. The dishonesty of having a married man as a lover for a time is certainly no worse, they feel, than the dishonesty of marriage for marriage's sake. Such a marriage would only fail anyway, and a failed affair is better than a failed marriage. In the meantime there are new experiences to seek, new men to know. Underneath there is often more than a little self-rejection by these women. They have set high ideals, and do not feel old enough or mature enough to live up to them. Often they benefit from seeing why the ideals have been set this way, as a cover-up for parental "failure," which in reality is no more than being human. They need permission to fail, to accept failure, in order to understand their self-rejection and the overstatements it produces. Some of them believe that if they were married they would only go on having affairs anyway, because they are still struggling to understand how permanent relationships in general are built. For them the perfect is often the enemy of the good, and they reject good relationships because they have been taught to find a perfect one. Just as many of the married people who have affairs are casualties of the myths about ideal marriage, so the unmarried with whom they have affairs are often casualties of the same myths.

Seen from each corner of the eternal triangle, then, the need to justify the lies and half-truths that protect an affair is frequently a product of expectations about marriage that are not tested by real discussion or open communication. The lies produce guilt. They are justified by the age-old mechanism of adapting attitudes to suit the private aims of the person concerned. Often the way this is done mirrors the early learning of the individual, the facts of life learned in the crucible of their own parents' marriage. But the guilt should not be overstated. It is amply compensated in most cases by the love that an affair makes possible, and that is valued, rightly, for its own sake.

CHAPTER SEVEN

One-night stands and multiple affairs

THE KIND OF ENCOUNTER in which two people meet for the first time, go to bed, and have sexual intercourse, then never meet again is called a "one-night stand." In some ways it is not an affair at all. There are seldom any emotional ties. The sexual side may be good, bad, or indifferent, but since the two people concerned never see each other again, there is no chance of putting it into proportion within a developing relationship. This one incident is seldom taken seriously within a marriage, and seldom reported. In one sense, of course, each one-night stand is a potential affair, and it is only because a particular liaison does not develop beyond the first encounter that it is classified as "sex only." At the same time, however, there is a sense in which the one-night stand is less likely to become a full affair. It is undertaken deliberately as a casual encounter. It has its own etiquette, its own procedures, and those who practice it have their own specially developed skills in procuring partners, pleasing them, and leaving them afterwards. In other words, there are experts at the techniques of the successful one-night stand, and a distinctive psychology usually lies behind their expertise. They may well see each incident as separate in itself, and as of very little importance because it was "just sex," but the married man or woman who takes part in a great many one-night stands is producing a definite pattern of behavior that is just as much a statement about personal needs and marriage as those made by married people involved in long-term "serious" affairs. It is therefore useful to look in some detail at the psychology of the one-night stand, and the people who are expert in them.

Mark, aged thirty-five, a very successful businessman, is of medium height, overweight, not particularly good-looking, but with a very direct and friendly gaze. He seems very much aware of the detail of other people's reactions, and is obviously determined and ambitious. His father was a serviceman, and his mother a teacher. He describes himself as "a spoiled brat when young"—an only child who attended prep school and public school. The interview with Mark revealed a long history of "casual sex."

> I first had intercourse at about fourteen. She was quite a bit older—all of two years. It was terribly exciting, but lousy in retrospect when I found out what it was all about. From seventeen to eighteen and a half I had a steady, but I would cheat on her if I was terribly attracted—in which case it would not be so much in order to gain another conquest as to try for a more mutual relationship.
>
> For me a conquest is basically being the catcher—it's the "kill" that is important, although I prefer not just to have casual "killings" but to have steadies as well. I like to have at least one steady in the background before I try for a casual.
>
> By the time I was married I had had about fifteen or twenty affairs—relationships lasting more than a couple of weeks and some of them several months. In addition there were many one-nighters—I have no idea how many women I have had. I married when I was twenty-four, and my wife was the same age. We come from slightly different backgrounds. She was a lawyer, and I was already achieving success in business.
>
> I quite enjoy being manipulated—then go along if I want to—but it was kind of a shock, once, to find that I had been

manipulated without being aware of it. It was a strange experience! Someone had gotten me into bed for a bet—strangely enough, a bet with another girl. I would probably have gone to bed with her anyway. But she was in control and I hadn't realized that. I have to be the one in charge.

Some of the women have mattered a lot. I lived with some for a while. I lived "in sin" with my wife for six or seven months at first—it was convenient. Then she put some slight pressure on me, and I did not want to lose her, so we married. We have two daughters, six and eight. I felt slightly more responsible, but even during the months we lived together before marriage I had had two or three other women—just things that happened. Two were just average, but one was very good. She and I were attracted as people and sexually. I still see her—three times a week, or not for a few months. She lives in Europe and is married. I would not live with her, but we enjoy each other a great deal and it is good in bed. Not very loving—more of a friendly sexual relationship. We don't mind parting—always "see you next month." It has been going on for ten years. I have no idea if her husband knows. I have met him twice and she has met my wife briefly. Occasionally, I get a card or a call. We meet at hotels. I like the meeting, but not for too long.

I enjoy conquests, all the different sorts. I might be by myself or with a friend, and there are two or three girls I could go for. So I go ahead. It is important to prove yourself to yourself. It's important to give her a good time, too, often at the expense of my own desires. I suppose basically I am insecure. I want to be certain that if she ever talks about it afterwards—and all women do—that it will be favorable. Men exaggerate, talk about women almost like objects most of the time. Women are more honest, I hope.

There are times when I find myself in bed with a woman I don't want. I try to perform.

And I risk compromising situations, too. I've walked into bars abroad and found someone I know there. It might happen to me one day, if it hasn't already done so. Invariably the gossip gets around. One day it's bound to get back to the wrong person. I would not like to be found out.

If she were unfaithful? Yes, I would mind. I would hate to think that there is someone else who had the power to get her into bed where he can manipulate her. I suppose I am reflecting my own male pattern.

If my wife had a one-night stand it might not upset me, but an affair would. I try to manipulate my wife so that she does not want affairs. I do this sexually, by convincing her that I am above average. If I thought she was having an affair I'd try even harder to keep her. I'd probably stop having women. But at present I don't get enough sexually or emotionally from my wife. A bad screw can be like masturbating—you feel empty afterwards—but I risk the bad ones for the gain of conquests. That's good for the ego.

Lucille is also in her thirties. Like Mark she works in business, but she is divorced and has one child, a boy of seventeen now preparing to go to college. She is warm and motherly with a dynamic streak that probably comes out as hard and calculating at work. She is not pretty, and has a small, dumpy figure, but she uses her eyes very effectively to show interest, and frequently modulates her voice into a sexually challenging drawl.

I married at nineteen to get away from home, had a baby the next year, and was divorced a year later. I was the third of three children, the only daughter, and spoiled to death. I was always expected to be pretty, to be the apple of my father's eye. He was quite shocked that I turned out to be so clever. Sex began when I was twelve, with an uncle who took me out sailing and had one hand on the tiller and the other up my skirt. He was great. We just sucked each other for a weekend until he went home with his wife and my grown-up cousin. There were always lots of boys. Some of them fell in love with me and had to be sent away or banned by my parents or theirs. One particular boy used to take me up into the attic in his house and never say a word, just screw me. He's a city councilman now—or was until a few years ago.

My marriage was the worst disaster, except for my baby. I tried to marry for love, but really to get away from home. When we met I kept up with two of my lovers for a while, but

I gave them up after I got pregnant. Yes, it was my husband's baby, I'm sure of that. I used to have orgasms while I was breast-feeding. But he also turned out to be rather violent, and it just didn't work out with him. We kept fighting and he left me.

After that it was rather difficult for a while. Men wanted me and I gave in to some of them, but I couldn't be bothered. I also discovered bisexuality. The baby took up a lot of my time. I had a good settlement, no real money problems, I suppose, compared with some, but getting a job was what helped most, financially and for my peace of mind. I got a nursemaid to live in, and a succession of cleaning women to come in a few times a week. One of them was terrific in bed. I still get cards from her at Christmas. She's married now, and has three kids.

Once I started work a whole new world opened up. I found I could get any man I really wanted—and believe you me, I wanted plenty! For some it was fun, for others therapy. I've met all kinds, shapes, sizes, and colors of pricks. I always tell them that it's beautiful, and very big, and they are great. If I don't want to go on into a full affair I say I'm still married and show them a photograph of me with my son. That cooled off quite a few of them. Their wives? I don't think about it. Once or twice, I have had big affairs. Mostly I regard an affair as one that lasts two or three months. It's not the emotional involvement—oddly enough I always feel emotionally involved to some extent, because people really do matter to me—it's the extent to which you look forward to seeing them again. I've had very good lovers who I'm sure just didn't like me in the end. But I've never chased anybody except for the casual one-night stand. Then I really do chase. They don't stand a chance. I size them up from the outside first, then just ask them to come to bed. Very few refuse, and those who do can always be persuaded.

Yes, there is an insecurity in my make-up. It goes right through everything I do, bringing up my son, financial needs and dependence on my father and my ex-husband, my job, everything. During the last year or so I've begun to tackle it, to get back into my past and to discover why I'm like this, through group therapy. I think I have to prove I'm pretty, even though I'm not really. My father always said I was. Not that my father could really have thought I was beautiful, but I still have a drive to show the world, all the fathers, that I am attractive and sexy.

I suppose I get a new man two or three times a week. I have no idea of the total; I lost count years ago. Some of them are very sweet. There was a shy little virgin recently who was due to get married this week. He asked me to the wedding, but I won't be able to get there. I let the men feel they're making the moves most of the time, but it is important to be one step ahead of them. I come very easily and very often with almost everyone, and if they are incapable I just relax and talk until they relax too, and feel reassured and then they can usually manage something. Sometimes I get girls instead. I've been to quite a few group-sex sessions as well. It's fun, and I don't have to take charge.

Underneath, I'm still looking for my real self. I used to think I would remarry, but I still feel afraid of falling in love and being let down. Being in love is fine, but falling in love would be a disaster. I need the control.

Vic, now aged forty-three, says he used to be an expert in the one-night stand, but gave it up some years ago when (as a result of a personal crisis in which his wife had an affair with a man who died of cancer) he and she developed a totally new and satisfying relationship. He married at twenty-two; she was nineteen and they were both virgins. During the first ten years of marriage he "lost count" of the number of casual, one-night relationships he went through.

My job meant traveling around a great deal setting up exhibitions and conferences in hotels all over the country. I was home only every other weekend, although I actually sent postcards almost every day—we still had them all till a year or so ago—and I called home every night. Many of the people I came into contact with were away from home only for a few nights, and looking for some fun. They were all shapes and sizes. I'm attractive, but not particularly good-looking—you can say I'm the teddy-bear type, cuddly. That appeals to a lot of women more than a handsome face and an athletic physique.

It began by accident almost. There was a married woman, one of the delegates, a dentist, who seemed very attracted to me. We talked and ended up in her room. She said, stay here and have some fun, so I did. It hadn't honestly occurred to me to see sex as fun until then. She had a hell of a good time, and I just laid back and enjoyed it. It scared me, I felt so guilty, but I couldn't tell my wife or she would have thought I did it all the time. I'll always remember that first one. Then there were others, just fun. I began to get the knack of spotting the most likely candidates, the ones who had promised themselves some action, a quick fling now that they were away from home. It seemed very easy at first. Perhaps I was just very lucky.

The first thing is to get the right person, someone who will feel flattered, and who is intelligent and mature enough to know what she is doing. I've had girls who just lie there like zombies, and who only do it out of desperation or depression. You sometimes end up doing nothing, and that's fine if you can talk, but not to have any exchange, any contact, that's no good. Sometimes you get the performing-seal type, the married woman with twenty years' anger and frustration to work off. They flip you over, and turn you this way and that, and laugh and cry when they come, and you cuddle them to sleep, and next day they go home satisfied. I'm sure many of them never do it again. Or perhaps that's my vanity.

You can usually tell who to ask. On a three-day conference they start looking around after noon on the second day, starting up conversations with the likely men, and flirting. They're like little girls let out of school, all eyes and legs. The conversation is light on the surface, but if you listen to the words they're often telling you frankly enough that they want some sexual excitement and see no harm in it. I always used to say I was married, ask them about their husbands, and listen. I mean really listen. You've got to do more than show interest; you must *be* interested. And you have to look after them, to be attentive: buy the drinks, and remember after a conference session what they said at coffee break, so they think, imagine him remembering that. Usually they'll give a hint or two that they love their husband but the sex is a bit stale and they need a change. I used to say things like: "Shall I freshen you up?" meaning either the drink in their hand or their sex life. If they got the point, they'd flirt back and let you know what they really wanted and how willing they were. The most fun often came from this sort of courtship. The serious side was the talk. I learned a great deal from them. I never went to college. Perhaps I should write a book—I will, one day.

The first day was the funniest. When we had something going with mostly older married women they all lived up at the pay phone, worried to death about their husbands and kids, asking if they'd cooked a proper meal, and swearing blind that he was feeding the kids baked beans and burned toast. It was a standing joke that none of the men back home could boil an egg. No wonder they were bored with them.

On the third night you usually knew who would risk it, who'd already had it, and who was going to bed with a headache. My best tactic was to leave the hotel bar with a likely lady and walk her around the block. Then, when the talk started to get interesting, I used to give her a chance to talk about sex and marriage and what she was like as a girl. A kiss and a cuddle in the bright lights, holding hands in the street, then, when she felt ready I suggested we go to bed, not to spoil the evening. Sometimes they made the first open suggestion. Once—but only once—one of them got her friend, and I thought she'd gone for a witness to get me arrested, but we had a threesome.

I enjoyed being good at sex—still do, of course. I suppose I learned with lots of women what I should have learned with my wife, but, as it happened, I learned that later, thank God.

There are certain rules, yes. Not so much rules as a code of conduct. You have to be clean. Be sure you check on contraception—in my experience the women seldom do. They have this thing, that it has to feel impulsive, and not planned. Women who use diaphragms at home leave them there so that the husband feels safe. I discovered this early—I went to bed and hadn't bought any rubbers because she was eager and I was sure that she would be safe. She was really upset when she found out. Then you have to use the right words. That's not easy. Some of them prefer the Anglo-Saxon, some the Latin. At first I didn't know half the words—perhaps they made up their own with their husbands—you know, "Would Mr. like to come inside Mrs.?" Later I used to find out when we got undressed. I'd tickle them and say, "What do you have here?" or "What do you call this little beauty?"

I think it's better to be honest about performance, too. I've read a lot of sex books, and I like the Chinese philosophy. Being close matters, not how energetically you can screw. They talk about "a thousand loving thrusts," not "a good lay." I go along with that. I used to be worried about performing, needed to be reassured. Later on, I suppose I gave more and asked less. The main thing is to talk, to get through the barriers so you're with a real person you can feel and respect. Once there was this psychiatrist—I'll always love her. She was a one-night stand and we never made love the way most men think of it. But all night long we loved and talked. I think she helped ever since, though I only met her the one time.

The technique of the successful one-night stand is not particularly different from that of any other successful seduction. One partner is ready and experienced, and selects, from the people available, those who seem most likely to connive at their seduction. The seducer prepares the ground thoroughly, being sure of having somewhere comfortable to go for love-making, providing stand-by contraception while hoping it will not be necessary, and presenting himself or herself as clean and interesting. Then the courtship procedure begins, with each person "shadow boxing," testing the other's readiness for the affair, and enjoying the other's company as far as possible for its own sake. This stage is the "hunt," in which the practiced seducer enjoys his or her own skill to the full. It may be less esoteric than Grand Master chess, but it is no less complicated and equally absorbing. The object of the game is to get the partner into bed, the "kill," and the sex after that is often less important. If it works, it adds another dimension of reward, but to many experienced chasers the "kill" is more important than the "feast." Mark clearly prefers to perform well so that the girls will give him a good report, but his love of the chase is his basic delight. Lucille says that she likes her men to think they have done the chasing, and

tries to surprise and thrill them with the sex. Vic in his heyday also
seems to have preferred the chase to the kill or the feast.

The difference between one-night stands with married people,
and the casual sleeping around of younger, single people, seems to
lie in the deeper challenges of the chase, and the greater probability
of a good feast. Vic discussed his views on this:

> I preferred the married ones, the first-timers. Many of them
> wouldn't dream of having an affair. Some of them never had
> an affair, and did dream about it. They were difficult, a real
> challenge. They often felt guilty and scared, sure their hus-
> bands would know they'd been with another man just by
> looking at them. You had to ease them into bed, like tickling
> trout, I imagine, though I've never done it.

Sex with an experienced woman was always, for Vic, more
fulfilling than with teenagers or people who had never had a long-
term stable relationship:

> It wasn't just that they knew what to do—there was more
> warmth in it, more tenderness, and more release when they
> finally let go. It might just be my vanity, but I often felt, and
> still do, that I was being let in on an important moment in
> their lives, a once-only experience.

For Mark, such considerations seemed unimportant, perhaps
because of his attitude toward sex and toward himself. A partner
was either "good" or "just average." He had far more difficulty than
Vic in talking about the details of sex, and he still had not come to
terms with many of his own needs, particularly his need to prove
himself over and over to be a real man. Mark gave the impression
of trying to demonstrate that he was a good salesman with a busy
schedule and his accounts to keep up. A good quick sale and a
measured amount of after-sales service was all he wanted, in sex as
well as business. It made no difference to him whether his partners
were married or not. As for his own marriage, this had scarcely
affected his sexual career. He gave the impression that the marriage
gave him the stability to feel safe enough to explore his instability,
and that if his marriage became threatened his answer would be to

perform better in bed, not to tackle the causes of his strange behavior. For Lucille, too, whether a man was married or not made no difference in principle:

> But it does make a difference, because each one is an individual, and I want to do something they will remember. A married man often has had very little experience outside marriage, particularly the older ones. I like to do things they don't usually do.

Both Mark and Lucille seem to fit one of the stereotypes, the view that the habitual one-night-stander is sexually promiscuous for neurotic reasons. Both talk of being promiscuous early in life, and of being spoiled as children. Vic said that he had a "reasonably happy" home life, as the second of three children, and he was a virgin until he married in his early twenties.

The drive to prove oneself sexually is a normal part of most people, and those who express this by having a long succession of casual partners are choosing an unconventional rather than a neurotic solution to a normal problem. Mark and Lucille began early. Vic was older when he started. Perhaps this helps to explain why Vic seems to have a more mature attitude toward sex and love, whereas Mark separates the two and, like Lucille, sees sex as manipulation for pleasure.

None of these interviewees was especially handsome or pretty, yet they apparently never lacked partners. To be beautiful in a conventional way is not the only form of attractiveness. All three had an air of confidence, and they exuded sexuality. All three were excellent talkers and listeners. It appears that they set out to please their partners, putting their own pleasure last, treating them with care and attention. At the same time, they moved in circles that ensured a continuous supply of willing partners who would share their own attitude toward sex. Murray's circle even included girls who would bet one another that they could get him into bed—although if this is read as fantasy rather than as fact it rings truer and says more about Mark than he would have wanted to admit.

Unlike stable, long-term affairs, the short-sharp informal quickie can be seen as an avoidance of the search for self-understanding. Many of the longer affairs discussed previously fitted into a personal-search strategy for the people concerned. The affair helps them explore their own attitudes and discover something about themselves. It is often a return to a search for identity after a period of marriage seemed to have ended the need for this. When the marriage goes sour, the individual starts to search again, going back to the point, often in late adolescence, when the quest was abandoned. The succession of one-night stands is not like this. Instead of setting up a single relationship in which two people can explore what they want from life, and what they can give as they get to know each other over weeks, months, or years, the successful one-night stand is an attempt to avoid commitment. It comes out as a pre-packaged parcel, perhaps with the surprise wrapped inside, but in many respects predictable. The seducer enjoys his or her own skill, and is reassured that the skill is still there. Then he avoids being committed and moves on to the next "victim." The objective is to do the same thing over and over again, and perhaps to do it more skillfully, but not to try something very different. The case establishes their identity as hunter or huntress, but it does little to help them develop beyond this.

Mark's comment on the possibility of his wife's having an affair is revealing: "If my wife had a one-night stand it might not upset me, but an affair would." His own life seems to be a succession of one-night stands. "I would hate to think there is someone else who had the power to get her into bed where he could manipulate her." So for Mark, at least, the business of sexual commitment in marriage has to do with power. He has the power to be the only person to possess his wife. Sex outside marriage also has to do with the exercise of power. Why would an affair upset him? Almost certainly because he has not yet managed to understand love as being a basis for real relationships, and he has a keen sense of the inferiority of his position, and of his powerlessness. Lucille showed a similar disinclination to relate to people beyond the casual encounter, and an equal concern for power based on a horror of being powerless. Vic, perhaps, was different. He seemed to relate more deeply, to be less of a performer. But he had the benefit of hindsight, and was probably no different at the time, the turning points being the night with the counselor, and his own wife's affair.

The man or woman addicted to one-night stands has many partners in quick succession. The multiple affair takes place when a married person has many affairs simultaneously. He or she may be, by all appearances, the well-loved and respected partner in a stable marriage and yet have, quietly tucked away here and there, enough lovers to spend every night of the week and several afternoons in bed with a different person. The following account illustrates some of the reasons for this, and some of the problems that arise.

I was particularly interested to hear about your study of extra-marital relationships, because as a social scientist myself it occurred to me that you might have great difficulty getting people to tell you about their secrets for fear of being thought boastful. This can arise from the way that those who have many affairs never tell, while those who have none or very few often boast of more than they have. For myself I have never boasted or talked about my affairs, although until recently I was involved simultaneously in as many as eight, as well as actively participating in a very happy marriage. I understand that eight might be thought a little excessive, but I assure you it is true. I do not wish to be interviewed, however, so the relevant facts from my point of view may not be of much use to you. However, for what they are worth, here they are.

I am in my mid-forties, a professor of graduate studies, married to an elementary-school teacher, and we have two teenage daughters. I was born in a small town, and I grew up there in the days before teenage sex was usual. There were six children in my family, of whom I was the second, and my father was a teacher who died when I was fourteen. In retrospect it seems a happy childhood, yet my parents fought long and bitterly, particularly over money. When my father died the family stayed together with help from the relatives, but things never seemed to be the same, and I felt that only I really missed him. Looking back I can see now that he had a succession of extra-marital lovers, a teacher from his school for a few years, a woman who ran an antique shop, and one in particular, a talented singer who was his lover at the time of his death. I can vividly remember her calling at our house when he lay in his coffin, and we went in together to see him. In my childlike way I knew she loved him more deeply than I did, and we clung together in that darkened room, she weeping openly, and me soft and silent and distressed. Later that year I found letters from her she had written in his last happy days before death, and I burned them secretly.

At fourteen I already had girlfriends, but no sex. That did not happen until after marriage, despite being overseas during the war and many chances to find out what it was like. I believed all the romantic stuff about saving yourself for the one true love in marriage. Also I was afraid of getting some-body pregnant, and yet utterly ignorant of how to do it. We were taught what rabbits did, and frogs, but not people. Most of my dating was done around the streets of my home town and on country walks. I was engaged soon after I was drafted, and I married almost as soon as my army "career" ended. The point of all this is that I never knew what interpersonal sex was all about until then, just endless masturbation on my own, and all the tremendous delights of kissing and cuddling. I fell in love many times between fifteen and eighteen. My wife was the one who listened best while I talked my head off. She waited for me, and I for her. It was the way things were done. We went to bed on our wedding night congratulating each other on having the good sense to admit that we were too tired and had better wait until the next night. However, we made it then, clumsily and tenderly, scared and proud, leaving a blood spot on the sheet that we had to soak out on the third morning. We were careful to always use condoms. It was a very long time in my marriage before I entered her with my naked penis, like discovering sex for the very first time, which I suppose it was.

The background of my marriage was the conformist way we courted, the influence of the extended family and all that went with it, and the provincial life we led for those first three years. This was in the late 1950s and early 1960s, yet it belonged easily to the early twenties. Our attitudes were really no different from those of our grandparents. I worked in a gov-ernment office, my wife in a factory. I read everything I could lay my hands on, and dreamed of a political career and going to Washington some day. Politics absorbed me more and more. We planned our first baby—my first time with no condom dates back to then—and shared all possible aspects of the pregnancy, reading all the right books. I tried to write, often working late into the night. I took correspondence courses. There must have been massive sublimation of sexual drive. During those early years I masturbated several times a day and made love to my wife nearly every night. She never knew I masturbated, just as, later, she never knew about my lovers. I spent much of my time with women and never noticed them.

Then I got a scholarship to this college to major in history and political science. We moved here with our baby daughter. Finances were grim. We fought over money, to my horror just like my own parents. The apartment was two rooms and a shared kitchen. I came home later and later. We had our second baby during that next year. College work was difficult, but I discovered a new talent for economics, and they liked my work. Sex was pushed to the back all the time. I began to overwork.

Discovering women was the next step, a true revelation that a different world existed. I had three consecutive affairs during my last year at college. It made me appreciate many things for the first time. My wife and children seemed more beautiful, not a burden, in a funny sort of way. One of the women helped financially. She came home for a meal, then to chat to my wife. For a few months she was part of the family in almost every respect, except that our sex life together was secret, though never furtive. What I began to realize was that being alive, loving, and sex were all natural.

I want to expand on this point. I was brought up to think of sex as something bad, to be controlled. Sex was dangerous to my father's generation and to the generations before. People controlled love because they had to control sex. My mother was probably a very shy woman all her life. She may have had six babies, but I doubt if she knew much about sex. It had always seemed to me that she thought having babies to be slightly unnatural and shameful. She hated her body, because her figure disappeared after her having babies. At one time she was pretty paranoid about it and wouldn't go out of the house because she thought that people saw her as disgusting. Her generation was probably all disappointed about sex. I expected to be disappointed by it. Love was something one was careful not to express too freely because it might lead to sex, and that would spoil a friendship. The unity of life, through our animal sexuality, and the joy and pain of it, that's the main thing.

I had a couple of short-lived jobs in management, then began to teach. Little by little I was collecting girlfriends. It was and is harder for me to relate to men. In my affairs I was reluctant to use people. The relationships tended to be long ones. Casual sex is of no interest to me. It is the love that I am seeking, to give and to receive. The problems are part of this. I have learned to weep. This living close to nature is wholesome. My own nature is not very different from any one else's, not more or less loving or stupid, and yet it is easy to escape from it into piety and conformity. I had affairs with anyone who stopped my escaping. Altogether there have been about twenty women in my life. Not many, by some standards, but often they were simultaneously there, giving mutual support and encouragement.

The eight came about this way. Three of them were very long-term affairs. One broke up last year after seven years of weekly meetings, often more frequent than weekly. She and I used to be determined to break up. She would have a casual affair, and confess, and once or twice, thinking we really had ended, I would find someone else (who lasted), often out of jealousy or just because I felt alone. So for about five out of the seven years with her I had three steadies. During one of those years I had affairs simultaneously with four more girls. One was a widow, one had a violent husband, another was a divorcee whose boyfriend was in prison, and the fourth was a student whom I met and went to bed with for the first time at a conference held in a convent, of all places!

Timing was difficult. The last two knew about my three steadies and were understanding, and friendly about sex. They both found other lovers eventually, and left me. I hate to think about it, but the V.D. risk was awful. I used to see my longest steady on Saturdays, my other two on Monday morning and Monday evening. That was partly due to their own work and the fact that my occupation gave me a free Monday morning. This left most of the week free. The widow had Wednesdays when her kids were out, and the woman whose husband beat her could only see me every three weeks or so. She used to write passionate letters instead. Every Tuesday I was home, and most Thursdays there were political meetings. The student and I went to bed after the meetings. Fridays I used to see the woman who had the criminal common-law husband. She was very much older than I, and very lonely, but kind and extremely sexy. If I got the chance I slipped in to see her most mornings except Mondays. She liked to hear about my problems with timing.

This did not last on such a scale for very long, only about a month or so, and happened about two years ago. There was one week when my wife was quite demanding and if I admit to a sneaking feeling of pride at being able to satisfy her as well as all my other lovers, this was honestly not what it seemed to be about. I loved all of them in many different ways. In some instances it seemed utterly cruel of me to cheat so often, yet all of them gained more than they lost, I think; I know my gain was immeasurable. The guilt I had came from having to suppress love, not from having too much. So many times the words would have come forth, promising more than I could give, had I not held them back.

I suppose it might help in your research if I try to explain why I have never told my wife about this. Frankly I do not think she would believe me, and I do not blame anyone who finds it all incredible. I am totally committed to her, and our love would survive the "infidelity." I do not feel unfaithful, or adulterous, or a betrayer. In time she would understand my need to explore these mysteries, but it would also make her very unsettled and jealous. In many ways it was purely unselfish, but the unselfish giving was to the other women, not to her. She would feel that she deserved all that love, though she has all the love I can give her, which is all the love I have.

It is because I have never told her that I do not want to risk an interview. You would probably try to psychoanalyze me in any case, and I do not want that.

My current situation may be of interest to you. I have two beautiful, steady relationships, one with an unmarried girl seven years younger, and one with a widow much older than

I am. I am in touch regularly with four other women whom I love very much and whom I meet from time to time—separately!—and sometimes make love with. We help one another, all of us, with problems, as good friends should. My closest partner is still my wife. Sex is different with each woman, and love is constant. They all know one another, except that my wife does not know about the sexual involvement. Perhaps together we have created a new kind of extended family. I'll leave it at that.

In some respects, the anonymous writer of this letter, like Mark, Lucille, and Vic, the one-night-stand experts, is a points collector, and plays the numbers game. His position, however, seems to be less of an escape, and more of a loving exploration. It is not possible to tell how typical he might be. There are no statistics on affairs, least of all on how many men and women have simultaneous affairs that are kept secret from wives and husbands. The irony, however, is quite clear. Casual affairs, for sex only, are not counted as serious. Serious affairs with several different partners at once, where deep emotional involvement and love play a major part, are frowned upon by society. What is loveless is acceptable; what is loving is rejected. Why are so many of us so afraid of emotional involvement, and so inept at understanding those who are less afraid?

CHAPTER EIGHT

Homosexual affairs

THE PEOPLE WE INTERVIEWED often seemed to be searching for new ways to make sense of their sexuality. They need to understand the power of sex, and how to give and receive love. Whether they are in their teens and twenties, or their thirties and forties, this is still the central developmental task of adolescence, the search for a satisfying outlet for sexuality. For one particular group of people, however, this normal search has an added significance. These are the homosexuals and the bisexuals. Their search involves not only a definition of the nature of the sex act and the role of love in sex, but also a definition of their own sexuality. Women who have love affairs with women, and men who love other men sexually, often have to find for themselves a way forward to their true feelings that cuts deeply into the accepted drift of society. Many begin to find themselves experimenting with their sexual unorthodoxy only after a conformist marriage. To their husbands' or wives' distress at the shock of an extra-marital affair is added the often deep distress of discovering that the spouse is homosexual, and that the "other woman" or the "other man" is the same sex as their spouse.

Widely accepted estimates suggest that ten percent of the population is undoubtedly heterosexual, another ten percent definitely homosexual, and that the majority vary to a lesser or a greater degree between these two certainties. Since, however, the society we live in is overwhelmingly dedicated to heterosexual marriage, it is hardly surprising that the majority controls and inhibits its tendencies toward homosexuality by a complicated arrangement of taboos, evident in all kinds of behavior, and emphasized further by the use of coarse jokes and casual flippancies about homosexuality. For example, men have their own ways of using the handshake and other forms of hand-to-body touching that avoid giving an impression of sensuality. The firm grip of a robust and manly handshake, preceded by a steady pressure of gaze and a careful choice of proximity (not too close!), avoids sexual ambiguity by exaggerating the characteristics of the stereotyped male dominant personality. Pressure and impact touching predominate. Caress touching is ruled out. Most men avoid the more sensual pleasure of hand-holding where other men are concerned, and when a handshake is mistimed and degenerates into an accidental hand-hold, men will often go out of their way to point out that they are unequivocally heterosexual. Among women the taboos against homosexuality are no less evident, despite a widespread fantasy among men that most women are naturally bisexual and would really prefer their own sex. When women meet and greet one another, kissing and cuddling are carefully timed, and the places that are touched are rigorously circumscribed, so that, just as much as men do, they avoid sensuality and merely exchange affectionate warmth. Women as much as men are wary of unintentional words and phrases that by innuendo might indicate homosexuality. Both greet such slips with bursts of laughter, to relieve the tension, and to provide an opportunity to reaffirm heterosexuality. One theory of humor is that it helps us deal with our innermost fears. If this is true, then the fear of homosexual tendencies is a significant part of the personality of far more of us than would admit to it. The fear is dealt with by surface frivolity. Violence and disgust lie behind the fear, and it can emerge to present a threat of terrifying proportions toward those who are led by their own emotional development to the conclusion that sexuality has for them unambiguously to do with loving someone of their own sex.

For many homosexual men and women, adolescence represents a severe crisis of identity that is submerged at the time by a heterosexual marriage. Ed, now in his thirties, was married at nineteen.

> Looking back on it, I can see that I got married mainly so that I could have kids. I had no romantic illusions about women. They did not turn me on sexually at all. I thought, it's the companionship of it that works, the sameness of men and women, and this discovery led me to try the usual quota of girlfriends until I found one who shared my love of cooking and home-making instead of seeing it as something to be used or derided. We married, and sex was so she could get pregnant. I felt it all for her, the whole process, the kickings of a moving baby, the pain of the contractions, the whole thing. I really felt that I should be having the baby, not her. It took a long time for us to realize that I was more woman than man. After the baby was born we might have made things work, but it went against her grain, and I was eating my heart out. To make a long story short, there was a crib death, poor little soul, and we broke up painfully and slowly as I found men to console me. Now I never even see her.

It is true also that Ed married to escape from home. His father was a professional military man, his mother the one person he most adored among her sex:

> Funny, but she can still not accept my homosexuality. For him there is no such thing as homosexual people, there are only homosexuals. When my daughter died they both helped to break us up. She took Jane, my wife, to her, and gave her a vacation, sort of, with an expensive private nursing home, gifts, and so on. Perhaps she, Jane, was the daughter my mother really wanted. It's vivid, still, fifteen years later. She's too good for you, she needs a real man. It was said in anger, but it still hurts. My father just smoldered and kept out of my way. I think he wanted to kill me. It took a lot of wandering before I found the way out. Now I'm part of a stable couple, every way a couple, except we can't have babies. I would like his babies, yes. But we don't talk about that!

Bobbie also faced many confusions, doubts, accusations of excess before she accepted her homosexuality. Now in her mid-forties, she married first in her late teens and again ten years later. At first she accepted passively the role of subservient partner. The relevation of the reality of her other sexuality came slowly.

> Marriage put me in a very defensive position. That is very common, but I did not know it at the time. Those "this is a terrific woman" remarks keep her in her marital place. Why I let it go on for so long I don't know. It was very humiliating to find out how much I had allowed myself to be humiliated. I was a wife in every way. I ironed shirts, vacuumed carpets, lugged shopping bags, cooked his meals. In the end he got a job abroad, and I simply said I wasn't going.

She had an affair almost immediately, still conventionally seeing herself as married to him, but tacitly rejecting the stultification of it all. The affair, like the marriage, was heterosexual.

> I went into it with my eyes open. He was a factory worker. He was the same as other men, except that intellectuals are less overtly chauvinistic. I prefer sexism that shows. I cannot stand being manipulated. Working-class men are less likely to do so, and when they do they are more open—coming out with comments like, "You are worth nothing, you bitch."

The affair lasted briefly and was followed by more of the same kind. Her husband announced the end of the marriage by telegram from Kenya, and she continued to choose men who ultimately would disappoint her.

> Sex in those days was a sudden screw, nasty, brutal, and short, as they say. I liked it in strange places, half dressed. The first man who wouldn't do that became my second husband. We parted amicably enough. There was nothing at all in it for either of us, and I could see myself heading once again for the missionary position and the ironing board. He never spoke his mind. His whole life was avoidance, of conflict, of work, of listening. It reached the stage where he could be witty only at my expense, so I left.

Bobbie's emotional development during these years had led her repeatedly to the same brick wall, that affairs with men only made her more intent on hurting herself, to prove her own worthlessness as a sexual being.

I decided I would no longer find men as I grew older. I now need women, infinitely more. I have been having a lesbian relationship for a long time. Women have not turned out to be second best. I am more at home, intimate, and relaxed than ever I was with men. I see my present lesbian relationship lasting. To some degree it is a mother–daughter relationship, but it is astonishing how much alike we are. She was always a lesbian, but I initiated the relationship. I sat with her one day, looked at her, and thought, "What a very interesting person." My sexual attraction has always worked like that. The relationship took a year to develop. Heterosexuality now feels wrong for me. If I had not discovered this I suppose there would have been a third marriage eventually.

Along with the common social defenses against bisexuality and homosexuality go several curious myths. One of these is that lesbians are simply women who can be "cured" by the attentions of a virile man. Another is that homosexuality in men is a form of illness that can be "cured" by a dedicated wife. Howard, a twenty-five-year-old, had been married for a year before he went to a therapist for help. "I was always bisexual, and after marriage the homosexual side became worse and it could get worse still. I'm deeply troubled that the marriage may not last."

His wife is Danish, an exceptional beauty. The couple worked in the same hospital. He was a technician, she a nurse, and before they married she went around with him, part of the "gay" scene. She thought she understood what it meant to be gay, and was flattered to be included in the group who, in her eyes, were gay in the old sense of the word, full of fun, lively, tender, glad to go to theaters and concerts. She looked around for the best of the bunch, and suppressed any conscious feeling of rescue in the romantic confidence of a whirlwind courtship. She married in the hope and the belief that his homosexuality would die a natural death in the constancy of the marriage bed.

A few weeks after the honeymoon, Howard began to go out

with his friends again, and this time she felt excluded. He now feels he married under false pretenses, but, like Ed, very much wants children. He loves his wife, but finds sex with men far more satisfying. To avoid the clash of interests, he changed his hours of work, and his wife went along with this, by taking a course of study that kept her out of the house in the evenings. Now, in the class, she has met lesbians for the first time. A couple of incidents upset her, and her attitude is hardening. The future of the marriage rests on a knife-edge of understanding and mutual caring, but the couple has perhaps already so avoided communication that dissolution is inevitable. Making their own rules would require of each partner more stamina in the face of the pressures of social conformity than either possesses.

In the case files of most groups that help homosexuals there are many similar examples of the way the homosexuality taboos of the majority deprive the minority of strength to develop unconventional solutions when one or the other partner accepts his or her own deviance. A slightly older couple than Howard and his wife, with a homosexual husband, encountered this suppressed fear and violence in its most direct form when the children of the marriage turned out to be sons. The wife's jealousy and anger surfaced, and she beat her children viciously before her own frustrations could be tackled. She was eventually persuaded to join a supportive self-help group, and through counseling she was led to understand why she felt so much disgust about sexuality that she had so hurt her own children. Gentle encouragement to explore her own body and to accept it through masturbation helped her deal with the rigid self-control her parents had unconsciously imposed on her, but that her husband's affairs had broken. Those in the group she joined were all wives of homosexuals who, having faced similar problems, could share her pain. She took a more interesting job and began to feel safe again in her own family, to the extent that ordinary things like vacations became possible again.

A few people have the looks and the talent to use a creative career as a way of finding people who accept their sexuality, whether it is exercised with their own or the opposite sex. One such is Tamara, a dancer, now in her mid-twenties:

> It was more a question of realizing that other people were not
> lesbian. My father was a decorator who ran his own business

while my mother kept a shop. She was the intellectual. He felt nothing very deeply, and always did as he thought. She had three of us. I'm the second, the rebel. We went to the local school in a small town. It was the sort of place where everyone knew about sex. I knew at eleven. The first time I heard the word *lesbian* was when I was thirteen, when someone used it to describe the girl I was having sex with. She was my eldest sister's best friend, and she had a kind of power over me. She instructed me: "This is how boys kiss." She started touching me. I remember my sexual feeling, and discovering the way I needed to respond to her. She moved away, but she wasn't the only sexual influence.

By the time I left school I had spent a lot of time trying to persuade school friends that they were lesbian too. I had to be active. I also had a relationship with a man. I still know him. I wanted my sex drive to be normal. I like men, but they just don't understand the satisfying relationship between women. I knew I was capable of enjoying sex, not frigid. I was very close to this man, a very nice person. We saw each other on and off from the time I was fifteen until I was eighteen and left school. All the time I was also having relationships with women.

My parents? They were very open-minded about sex. They thought it was a phase I would grow out of if they didn't . make a fuss. They never used words like *homosexual* and *lesbian*, so I thought it had never occured to them. I thought of myself as bisexual. Suddenly I realized that this boy and I were supposed to be getting married. My father said he would build us a house, and at that moment I realized, a sudden thought, I'd see the boy every day. A future of that! I loved him, enjoyed having sex with him, but it would stifle me. It could not work. I got out of it.

Before that, when I was about seventeen, I had had my first married Casanova. I thought it all very amusing and secretive. It didn't occur to me that his wife had feelings. At first it was just a casual fling for him, flattering, rejuvenating. He was about forty-four, boyish, immature. He began to talk about divorcing his wife. He had four children. I think it started because he wanted to prove he was still attractive to girls.

At this period Tamara began to experiment not just with her own sexuality but with the power it gave her to make men and women behave in silly, irresponsible ways. She comments:

> I found out at the time that I could get him to do anything. The sordidness of it appealed to me. I put a head scarf on to disguise myself, and we would sneak around to his friend's house, or do it in the car. I told my friends he was married. I was a young girl wielding my power, and the more power I wielded the more womanly I felt. At the time I must have needed this.
>
> I used to flirt a lot—I just wanted to make man weak. I don't know if it was so much to do with sex as politics. It was a mixture, rationalized partly as politics. I had a real resentment of the way girls were treated, still have. My brother got out of doing the dishes. My father "talked" to men, but my mother was only credited with "chatting" when she talked to women. The place I grew up in was full of intolerances of women.
>
> What I had discovered is that men are sexually weak, ruled by sexual drive. They can be totally distracted by a girl with pretty legs. Men are physically stimulated easily, and for a long time I flirted wildly with them but kept my serious, my loving relationships for women only.

Two of the women Tamara met for lengthy affairs were married. By then she had moved away from home and into her chosen career as a dancer, managing to avoid some of the more obvious pitfalls while using her considerable beauty to attract and maintain the attention of influential people.

> I didn't realize at first that the first of these was married. We met while on vacation. She had a villa on the Mediterranean, and I was there with a man. She was also called Tamara! She was in her fifties. I think I satisfied her maternal and her sexual needs. Maybe she really wanted to make love to her daughters. They were older than me. I don't think they know about her bisexuality. At first I thought she was paying me attention out of attraction to the man I was with; then, one afternoon at siesta time, she stood and watched while he and I had sex. She

was hidden behind a big white arch and saw that it did not work; the sex with him came off very badly. I think I guessed or hoped she was there, and we just looked at each other and went to her room. The following year she invited me and paid my way. I found it very exciting. No one would have known. People would have thought she was my mother. We *knew* each other, in the full sense of the word.

Although as far as this affair was concerned there was no problem with the husband, the young dancer still found a family drama to relate to. She recalled her feelings about the daughters, their "snootiness," which she inwardly laughed at. In all other respects she was accepted almost as another sister. Was she attracted to them sexually too? She felt she might have been, but had not pursued it. One factor—another element in the drama—was her lover's obvious jealousy. It would have hurt their mother in very subtle ways for her to have seduced the daughters. Perhaps they might have guessed too accurately why the young Tamara was so popular with the older one.

My second married affair was with a girl from one of the suburbs. I met Joanne at a disco. Again, I did not know she was married, so that did not motivate me. She was very attractive—sophisticated, tall, well built, always suntanned with an athletic body. She moved like a businesswoman. We went back to her place. It took hours in the car—my mistake, because I thought it was near the city! Then she said we had to be quiet. Her husband would be in bed. I thought she was setting me up for a threesome. We slept together on a couch. I don't think he realized. Sunday lunch was embarrassing, to say the least. I came back here by train.

She began to visit me. She had always seen herself as heterosexual. She was very nervous of being seen in bars and the like with me. But we had sex together. She was very passive. It went on for about four months. Her husband found out and used to play it down. He felt very inadequate, a nice man who spent his time trying to make advances toward me, while I tried to play it down. Finally I said: "I'm interested in your wife, not you."

Lots of men like their wives to have women lovers. I tried a threesome once, but it did not turn me on—it was very distracting.

The sexual thing is not that important so long as there is some communication. Men don't think women can get off with women. If they realized just how much a threat it was they'd be less complacent. Some of them simply say, "Have my wife, so long as I can watch."

Tamara says that her work keeps her unsettled, rootless. She says this suits her temperament, allows her to meet people who value sexuality and respond readily to sexual overtures. Yet it is often lonely—not just the cliché loneliness of empty motels on tour, or the uninvolving casualness of a succession of strange bodies in her bed. Her work is her life—spontaneous, demanding, and based on the need to stay close to her sensuality. That demands a kind of sacrificial loneliness, one that is based on the need to stay intuitive and spontaneous, not to settle into a long-term rhythm with familiar people who could know her too well. Yet she needs people she can turn to, who make no demands.

For the past few years I have had a regular friend—regular when I'm at home. We spend nights together, but we are not monogamous. In fact last year I had an abortion. He is an old friend who does me a favor when I feel sexually frustrated. I'd had a coil fitted, but it let me down. I don't hate men. Unfortunately I'm very fertile. Next time if I have sex with a man who turns me on, the sex at least won't be spontaneous.

Yet there are still conflicts, the need to defend homosexual outlets, while heterosexuals do not seem to have to defend their style of expression.

If two people have sex together, then there shouldn't be any boundaries. In practice I'm not particularly sensitive internally. Anyway, fingers can bend and do so much more. Often someone can see a feeling between two people even when they are not connected, in contact with each other at any intimate level. The potential for intimacy shows. They suddenly become nervous with each other, they can't put their arms around each other. Sad!

If a woman has accepted the traditional roles it would take a lot of strength to throw them overboard. In theory most women can manage to love men or women sexually. But there are these feelings, on the one hand of inadequacy, not being quite a woman, and on the other, guilt. The real person is squashed in the middle. Society resents bisexuality. It's as though it is naked greed to want both. Society hates this burning of the candle at both ends, and jealously gets you for it.

I wouldn't accept marriage in the traditional sense. If I lived permanently with anyone it would be with a woman. Women are more tender, and sympathetic. It's difficult to define this. Both sexes are so indoctrinated.

Tamara rejects guilt. Other people, she says, try to make her feel guilty. She sees her intellect as the saving quality, since, as a very pretty woman, she has always had to cope with other people's attraction to her, even as a young teenager. At first it made sense because, with other women, she could feel safe and involved without physical violence forming an element in the passion that was directed toward her. Other pretty girls she knows had less luck, less strength. Their beauty frightened their parents, so they abdicated responsibility and left their daughters prey to every man who came along.

I was lucky to realize how much of a hold I could get over men. It helped me to learn to be strong. Being intellectual and pretty has made me confident, a winner. I seek lively minds, creative minds with a strong sense of identity.

With women you can't fake an orgasm, and passion when it happens is sensual and full, not a trial of strength and submission to superior muscle power. Sex with another woman is very natural. I like the feel of a healthy body, the touch of skin, the layers of soft flesh under it, the shape of the bones, lightness, gentleness. Foreplay is all of it. There is no rush to get anywhere—yet if the feeling is sexual, there is an objective. Most people take sex too seriously—or it suddenly becomes very serious in the middle. It is different if you are in love.

A man making love seems to turn off when he's finished—he may even turn over. Women are oriented to hugging and kissing. If I have an orgasm I'm full of well being. I want to radiate to someone I've had it with.

Through her work as a dancer, Tamara explores creatively the sensuality that defines her identity. Her bisexuality is an expression of her whole self, a reaffirmation, as she matures, of her need to be autonomous. For many less fortunate individuals, the need to discover a sexual role that feels right still has to be met. The sexually deviant, as opposed to the merely unconventional, often marry in a bid for "normality," and fail to achieve it. Mary is thirty-five; her husband is thirty-seven. His attempt at orthodoxy was also an attempted escape from his penchant for punishment as part of sex:

It's just that I can't help him, sexually. But that doesn't mean I don't love him, don't want to help. Beating him sickened me. He's a quiet, meticulous man, gentle. He has many good qualities. We seemed to enjoy sex at first, but later it became rarer. He admitted his homosexuality from the start.

The relationship works at a practical level. She is the home-maker, but he also cooks and shops.

I understood it eventually. Out of the blue I found I had fallen for another woman. I kept quiet. Then we found that we worked in the same building. Eventually I told her and she went berserk, screaming, shouting, putting me down.

The similarities brought them together, through a form of acceptance and a large measure of companionship. He still has to find relief outside the marriage, and so does she.

I'm still looking. It seems unlikely that I'll find who I want, whether man or woman. But he still matters most. We have a laugh together about it, as an odd couple. If only people knew

they would be horrified. Yet if they really knew, really understood, they'd only find two ordinary people with a not too
unusual, ordinary problem.

Gordon is fifty. His behavior is marked by odd rituals and
deep humility. He married twenty years ago, but the marriage has
never been consummated, because of the unreasoning terror that
seizes him whenever he nears the point of "normal" sexual intercourse. A succession of convictions for indecent exposure has utterly
humiliated him. His wife doggedly persevered until last year, when
a young male friend, a social worker, began to develop a close
relationship in an attempt to help him. Gordon maintains that he is
totally heterosexual.

He just wants to help me accept myself. He encouraged me to
admit my sexuality, and when I did so, he congratulated me.
This was not public, you understand. We did it in his bedroom,
just the two of us. I took a lot of persuading. I let him
masturbate me. But it is not a homosexual relationship. Neither
of us is homosexual. He's trying to help me, that's all. But my
wife cannot, I'm afraid, accept this. She is convinced that he
is a queer, as she calls it. It made her very jealous.

His wife could live with his criminal record, his odd gentleness,
his strangely diverted sexuality. But she could not take this ultimate
deviation, this inner conviction of hers that he was now becoming
homosexual. She walked out. It would not have been acceptable to
leave him before, a man in trouble with the law. People would now
understand his being abandoned, after twenty years of getting
nowhere with him, if they could know this about him. There are
many explanations for her final acceptance that the marriage has
ended, but there is no doubt that one major element is her horror
of homosexuality.

Because the majority defends itself in such skillful and complex
ways against the tendency, people who are homosexual still live in
a world of overt denial. They may accept covertly that there are
many like them, and "come out" socially into the world of events
and selections where partnerships are made and unmade. Many do
not "come out," but still accept their own homosexuality. When

they form partnerships they behave as all couples do, falling in love, agreeing to be exclusive to each other, joyfully and seriously committing themselves to a lifetime of mutual emotional development. Like married heterosexual people, they live together, but they may drift apart into private affairs. The ones with plain faces have a difficult time just like heterosexual people, because they find partners harder to obtain. The pretty ones, like all pretty people, find that sex is easy to get, and love is far harder. For the ten percent who will always prefer their own sex, the problems of extra-marital affairs are no different from those faced by married heterosexuals. They deserve the right not to be singled out for further special mention.

CHAPTER NINE

Re-awakening

IT IS SAID THAT YOUTH IS WASTED ON THE YOUNG. During the teens and twenties and, for many, until well into the forties, sex and love are very often the source of turbulence and distress. These are the years when, according to the traditional view of beauty, women are at their most attractive and men their most handsome and energetic. These years are dominated by falling in and out of love, having babies, getting and staying married. Affairs during the twenties, thirties, and forties are very often there to complete an adolescent sexual agenda, to work through those tasks of childhood that circumstances have left uncompleted, and for which new opportunities are presented by chance meetings. By forty the fresh bloom of youth has usually gone. Faces and bodies are marked by the experience of childbearing, problem solving, getting and spending. People begin to look *who* they are, to show their maturity, often to feel that passion is misplaced, and that at last they can understand love and keep sex in proportion.

For those in their fifties, sixties, and seventies who stayed married to one person while children were born and grew up, middle age is often a period of reawakening. An affair at this stage may well bring even more stability to a stable marriage, enabling one partner to feel alive in new ways without in the least threatening the other. For the older woman particularly, there can be a reversal of the psychological aging that so often accompanies an awareness of physical changes. Her sex drive need not—often does not—diminish, while that of her husband often does. The dilemma is well illustrated by the following letter:

> I thought you might possibly be interested in my little story. I won't bore you with the details, but just to put you in the picture will tell you that I am seventy (seems impossible!) with a kind, devoted husband to whom I have been married for forty-five years, and whom I would never wish to hurt or humiliate. We had a good sex life for twenty-five years, but not much sex after that, which I have found hard to bear, though I could not now even contemplate having sex with my husband. We have our own bedrooms and live a decent life— in fact I think for my husband it is a completely happy one. I conceal my feelings pretty well, though I get depressed at times. I have just been through a "low"; perhaps that is why, selfishly, I am writing to you as a sort of therapy.
>
> > Best wishes,
> > Yours sincerely,
> > (signed) S.A.
>
> I think I will mail this immediately; by tomorrow I might decide not to.

S.A.'s dilemma is that she has no lover, and her shame and frustration are such that merely to write down the problem brings a kind of relief. But for some, a more effective therapy comes through seeking and finding a lover, in the form of a younger man.

What are the special features of such older–younger relationships? One characteristic is that such an affair is often a reaction to aging itself rather than to marriage. Jo's story illustrates these and other points. She is in her early sixties, a professional woman in a senior position at the peak of her career, has a grown-up son and lives in a large city in the Midwest.

It's almost impossible to say why or how an affair starts, and for me, and probably for most people, it was unsought, and in a way unwanted.

I met this man several years ago. He was more than thirty years younger than I am. We were at a business conference, and although I had seen him before I had never looked at him as a person. On this particular occasion he made a point of seeking me out and complimenting me. I suppose I *was* flattered. What woman of fifty-eight—almost fifty-nine—would not have been by the attention of an extremely attractive young man of twenty-five? It wasn't so much what was said as the way he looked at me, and it was fun and exciting and good for my ego after years of faithful, dutiful wifehood.

Shortly after this he asked me to have dinner with him, and I accepted, my feelings a mixture of excitement and nervousness. I invited him in for coffee when we came home. My husband was away. Nothing happened until he was leaving, when he kissed me, and I found myself responding almost against my will.

Almost two weeks later his wife was away and his small son was staying with his mother when he invited me down for coffee one evening. I went knowing that I would eventually be unfaithful (for that is what I had been brought up to believe that extra-marital sex means) to my husband for the first time, and not quite sure that I wanted my middle-class conventional lifestyle to be upset in that way.

After several days of indecision and mental turmoil, I stopped making excuses and went to bed with him, still feeling full of guilt. I found it very difficult to appreciate that another man could find me sexually attractive, and almost unbelievable that such a very attractive young man could do so. He could probably have had any girl he wanted. How could he possibly find a woman so much older attractive in any way at all? In all honesty I cannot say the sex was particularly good, exciting in a way, but in no way as satisfying or fulfilling as sex with my own husband.

Shortly after that he went abroad for a year. He left without saying goodbye, and that really did hurt. I can still remember the bitterness and depression that followed. However, he did this much for me: He made me look at myself really closely, and I didn't like what I saw: a middle-aged, conventional wife, a bit overweight, etc. I lost weight, went through my closet, had my hair cut short, and decided to have some fun. Which I did, quite successfully, for the next year. I would never have believed that there were so many attractive young men who found older women attractive. I must have been walking around blindfolded.

Then one day, out of the blue, the man who was responsible for all this came back into my life, still interested and only too willing to restart where he had left off. By now I was no longer the inhibited, slightly guilty woman he had known before, and sex between us was good and exciting. He was out of work for a few months, so we were able to spend afternoons in bed together. It was fun, it was satisfying, in every way, and I cared deeply about him. At the same time my relationship with my husband improved. It had always been good, but now in some way it had an extra quality, as though I had at last realized my own sexual potential, which had until then been dormant.

I still know and care about him, but our relationship has developed into a deep friendship, with little emphasis on the sexual side. We both know that we can turn to each other for help in all sorts of ways. It was wonderful, and I shall always be grateful to him. I wonder if he realizes just how much he has done for me, how much richer and fuller my life is now.

I have since met the man who is now my real lover, and he too is younger than I am, but to me is someone so special that I cannot imagine life without him, and who has shown me what "loving" really means.

I suppose really that what has occurred in the last ten years is that I have allowed my natural, but firmly suppressed sexuality to blossom again. I was not brought up in a repressive home, and although I was warned about the dangers of pre-marital sex (and very real they were in those days) I did have some sexual affairs before marriage. Looking back, I don't know whether this was wise or not.

Since having my first real affair I have found out that several of my own friends are also having very satisfactory affairs, although I appear to be the only one with a lover who is younger. I've been told I look ten years younger; I certainly feel like a teenager at times. I'm more sympathetic to other women who have affairs.

I don't believe that what I am doing is wrong in any way. Love is something that cannot be confined or caged, but it has to be love, not just sexual gratification. I wish every woman could have what I have found—I don't deserve it, but I have two beautiful men who between them satisfy all my desires completely. Perhaps my lover feels that way too. I don't know. But I do know that at last I feel I can be me after years of being someone I thought I ought to be.

You asked me to comment on the idea that younger-men–older-women relationships were based on the man's seeking a mother substitute. It depends very much on the people concerned and, of course, I can only speak here from personal experience. In my first affair I was probably, certainly at first, very conscious of the age difference, but I still looked at him as a very desirable man, not as a son. I knew he liked older women, he had in fact told me so the first time I went out with him. I said something one afternoon when we were in bed to the effect that perhaps he was looking for a mother and that maybe to me he was another son, to which he replied, "Some mother!" Shortly before my birthday, when I was having coffee with him, I said I was old enough to be his mother. I happen to know that she is the same age as I am, and he said, "If you were my mother I would believe in incest." I don't think, though, that I feel myself to be in any way a mother figure to him, and I'm also sure that I don't feel *that* way about *my* son. Age has its compensations and, while one loses the freshness of youth, maturity brings with it many other gifts. Not that I claim to be all that mature. I'm still learning and growing in many ways.

My son's friends think I am about thirty-nine. So far I have had little need of artificial aids to stay young. Perhaps being loved so beautifully is all that is necessary. I do, however, watch my weight and exercise regularly. I'm lucky in that I have a fairly good figure, a supple body, and very few gray hairs. I hope to stay like this for the next ten, fifteen, twenty years. In some ways that is up to me, but I would also like to have both my beautiful men with me as well, and that is something that is outside my control. My first lover gave me the incentive to do something about myself, besides opening the doors of the cage. The incentive to stay that way is so much stronger now, not just because I want to be beautiful for my lover, but because I feel so much better and enjoy life so much more. I intend to live life to the fullest in the years left to me.

I still suffer agonies of indecision—at times torn between the longing to be with my lover at every available opportunity and the necessity to lie at times in order to do this. Just occasionally I get to the point where I feel that it would be so much easier to opt out, but I can't; I love him and need him and want him desperately. I don't want to live without ever seeing him again, or hearing his voice. However hard it is at times, I wouldn't change anything.

In her account, Jo touches on three important themes of general relevance to affairs that take place late in an otherwise conforming marriage. The first of these has to do with aging and with physical beauty. Because we live in a culture in which youth and beauty are thought to go together, young people are often thought of as more beautiful than older people. According to some psychologists who specialize in the study of attraction, even those young people who are seen as unattractive are victims of this because their bodies look older. Many women apparently accept that once they reach forty they are unlikely to be seen as sexually attractive. They expect by fifty to look less attractive. And yet a woman's sexual drive very often increases once menopause is over and she has accepted that the fertile years of her life are at an end. Now she can enjoy sex for its own sake, spontaneously and with no fear of pregnancy, if only she has a man who finds her attractive, whom she loves, and who is an exciting, compatible partner. By their mid-fifties most women are through menopause, often, today, with none of the worst symptoms—the headaches and hot flashes—that their parents had to face in the old days, because of the modern use of hormone-replacement therapy. The traditional idea of marriage, however, was that by then most women would have long ago given up sex, that a career of pregnancies and infant deaths would have long ago turned them from lovers into mothers, and that they should not only be grandmothers by this time but look appropriately shapeless and sexless. Today, however, not only is menopause a new beginning for sexuality rather than an end to it, but women are having fewer babies during their fertile years, receiving better ante- and post-natal care, eating better, suffering fewer infant mortalities among their children, and keeping their figures and complexions. Women live longer and retire earlier than men. Now, when a woman reaches fifty-five, she can often look forward to another twenty years in which her sex drive may not diminish, and during which she will look a great deal younger and sexually more attractive than the vast majority of women of that age in previous generations. The older she gets from this point, moreover, the fewer men there will be to choose from among her contemporaries. In 1970 there were 475 widows for every 100 widowers. By 1978 the ratio had become 545 per 100. Remarriage in later life to a contemporary is less likely. In the meantime, at the younger end of the population, there is now a surplus of men. Under these circumstances, what would be more natural than an increase in liaisons—illicit or solemnized—between relatively younger men and older women?

> May I, as a husband in his fifties who struggled successfully against extra-marital relationships for more than twenty years of happy marriage, offer a few thoughts and an experience of a relationship that hopefully has done no harm, and probably much good to two people?
>
> I think that anybody who has been married for twenty years and never tried another partner must be terribly curious. But from my experience it is the emotional affair that is damaging; emotion drains from one relationship (the marriage) to feed the other. And I think that men, and women too, who leave one partner, and perhaps children, are terrifyingly wrong if the reason is a stronger emotion than one feels for the original partner. And, let's admit it, this happens all the time. It's so wrong, and wasteful of people's lives; probably more to be condemned than anything else because of the hurt it willfully inflicts.
>
> On the other hand, a sensible liaison, if you can find that strong a character, is probably likely to do far less harm to anyone if you can keep it completely and utterly under wraps.

After all, you don't tell anyone you are having a satisfying relationship with your wife. So why bother anyone with details of the extra-marital thing? It would possibly cause more trouble than it is worth.

Doubtless, extra-marital affairs are almost exclusively motivated by selfishness, but self-interest is hardly to be denied from anything sexual, as the mainspring is a human, *i.e.*, physical and emotional response.

I did find such a character, and lucky for me. At an age when many men are making fools of themselves by gaping at and pinching the office girls, I met an older lady who, not without some qualms, allowed me to become her surrogate husband while she looked for a new partner to replace a husband who had left her for a younger woman, and it did us both a world of good.

She was sixty-three and I was fifty. And I would advise any middle-aged man not to spurn the chance of an older mistress if all other circumstances are right.

Men are foolish to think that only women with young or youngish bodies can excite a man to a high level of passion. A sagging breast and a varicose vein are of absolutely no importance.

Margaret is a pretty, lively, and intelligent woman. Her character is such that she has strong principles about not harming a marriage. She suffered too much when her own husband deserted her at sixty.

She and I met through business and knew each other for two years before we did anything at all. She has her own home in a suburb of a northern city, a good income, and no predatory instincts at all except that she was at the time lonely, and I agreed to help her find a husband.

This has been a serious search for an intelligent person, because she had a lot to offer, and still has. At the time I was having problems myself, pressures that many middle-aged executives have, and I will be frank and say that what I wanted was a haven where those pressures were totally absent and hardly likely to be allowed to remain in my mind at all.

I didn't want to risk having a diversion with someone who was herself a risk to marriage, and Margaret didn't want to risk an affair with anyone who was going to interfere with her plans. But we each knew that the other represented a potential answer to a problem that was not going to be permanent.

Margaret was married at twenty-six, and enjoyed a happy sex life with her husband for over thirty years. When he left her for another woman she had never had another man's hand on her in her life. After she recovered partly from the bitter shock, she decided to have, as she put it, "some fun, before it was too late."

She did have a lover, if one can use the word, in this context. She had a married friend whom she slept with one night every few weeks. He had a wife who he said was incapacitated by arthritis. Thus this friendship was doing him some good. But it was not doing her much good because he suffered from such premature ejaculation that it was hardly worthwhile.

Thus, I suggested to Margaret that she and I become sexual partners once a month until she found a husband.

We were determined not to upset anyone. In fact she used to give me quite stern lectures on the lines that it was terribly cruel to hurt a wife, as she had been hurt.

Thus we began a relationship that nobody knows of. Telling your friends is something you simply don't do. We figure we both got a great deal of benefit out of the warmth of simple enjoyable love-making with no strings, and no prospect of betrayal.

I would call at her house once a month, usually in the afternoon, around 3 P.M., with a briefcase under my arm, admiring the roses on her neat lawn.

She would receive me at the door graciously, and the neighbors' curtains, if they twitched, would hardly conceal suspicious folk.

Then we would have a cup of tea, or a drink, and about 3:30 P.M. go into the back bedroom, which had a superb view of the countryside. We would simply drop our clothes on the floor, and mount each other with happy satisfaction on her daughter's bed.

This might sound a bit crude. But it was what we both

wanted, and enjoyed. We felt a bit guilty the first couple of times, and particularly she, with a lifetime of "respectability," and many qualms about sharing her body with two men.

But for two years we exchanged affectionate therapy, once a month. The other man, who was sixty-eight, unfortunately died. She had a traumatic time after that, and one or two false starts toward relationships with men who were just not compatible. She said that older men did not want marriage, just someone to cook for them and put them to bed!

A month or two ago Margaret met a very nice man of sixty, and, though she is now sixty-six herself, we hope she is either going to marry him, as they are so well suited, or form a long-term relationship.

She has asked me to be present at the wedding, if it takes place! I would be delighted. I think she deserves some happiness.

In two years, Margaret was a perfect mistress. She never called me at the office, or at home. She made no demands. She rarely refused me a visit, and only occasionally declined to have relations.

She says I did her a great deal of good, boosting her morale as a younger man, ridding her of prudery in the sexual sense. This gives me enormous pleasure, because a one-sided, grabbing relationship is not what I wanted. Though a demanding one wasn't either!

I found the affair soothing and exciting at the same time, and hopefully it has been an enormous health benefit.

Margaret would lecture me on never allowing my wife to be hurt, even in the act of intercourse! I must say I regard her as one of the best friends I ever made in this life, and have nothing but affection for her, as she has for me. I have a lot of respect too. If there were more like her, the world would be a happier place.

I guess you don't want clinical details, but as a lover she was considerate and superb. I suppose the neighbors would be shocked to think that she had straddled me, *Peyton Place* style, behind drawn curtains in the sunny afternoons. But I think we saved each other from depression by temporarily and discreetly abandoning the old morality.

My advice to any man in the same position would be: never hurt your wife . . . and choose a sympathetic older woman.

The second general theme is the conforming marriage itself. In a society where marriage predominates, the extra-marital affair tends to be seen as an ugly, regrettable period of doubt and pain when one marriage fails and another begins. It is all very unfortunate, but the peal of wedding bells wipes out the pain as another union is celebrated and the new couple start to live, at last, happily ever after. The yardstick of success in marriage tends to be the number of years it lasts, and silver, golden, and (especially) diamond wedding anniversaries are regarded as occasions for congratulation. On the face of things, conforming and faithful marriages work extremely well. Certainly a marriage that has lasted thirty years is unlikely to be seen as anything but stable and successful. The companionship of the couple, the shared experience of conquering problems together during that time, and the loving friendship that develops from sexual exclusivity over so many years are often self-evident. For a vast number of people this completeness of a union with a member of the opposite sex offers the necessary security for all the richness they would ever expect to gain from the sexual side of their lives. They enter marriage in order to experience it and to face life's difficulties with somebody constant at their side.

In most cases, people also marry to settle down, have babies, and see them grow up and marry. But what happens when these tasks are complete? Do they then just face the remaining years by quietly tending the garden and knitting sweaters? Their achievement is history, and nothing they can now do will spoil it or take it away from them. The pressure is off. They can have some fun, perhaps, just enjoy themselves. Yet, for many, this is no answer at all. Life has been spent facing difficulties and overcoming them, coping with emotions, and learning that a rich and varied life is quite a different matter from one that is placid and carefree. By "living again," many men and women in their fifties, sixties, and seventies mean facing new problems and challenges, not retiring from life and waiting patiently for death. To feel young again means to experience some of the turmoil of youth through the nerves of maturity. Their long-term sexual partners long ago exhausted the repertoire of sexual discovery. With a new and younger partner the exploration can be exciting and refreshing, and the achievements now completed within the conforming marriage are not threatened. An affair at this stage in life is a new challenge with fewer of the worries that would have haunted affairs earlier in marriage.

Third, age differences seem less absurd in couples once the traditional basis of marriage changes from childbearing to sexual partnership. The marriage of an old man of seventy to a sixteen-year-old girl will still arouse comment, as will that between the septuagenarian lady and the teenage boy. These are extreme cases, of course, and they arouse such a reaction in the media partly because they suggest the absurdity in an extreme way of the young girl's having babies by an old man, and the impossibility of the young man's having children by the old woman. There must, then, it is thought, be another reason for such liaisons: The old man must be perverted, or the young girl is after his money; the old woman needs a son, and the young man is after *her* money, or is afraid of sex.

It is interesting, however, to look at the point where differences in age become less extreme. The dividing line lies in that zone where one partner is "old enough to be your mother"—the position Jo found herself to be in with her young man—or "twice your age" when the girl is younger. A difference of twenty years or so produces this effect, yet only when one partner or the other is still comparatively young. The older people are, the less age differences arouse comment. Differences of ten or fifteen years are far more noticeable in the teens and twenties than they are in the fifties, sixties, and seventies. Over the age of sixty, a twenty-year gap would pass unnoticed.

Once sex is acceptable as not being predominantly for the production of children but for the building of an exciting, loving, and satisfying relationship, it becomes easier for society to see that age differences make very little difference sexually. In fact, they probably make no difference at all. Beauty is not solely to do with youth, and sex is not something that stops at forty. The fact that two people may be of widely different ages can, like any other difference, make them more interesting toward each other, and more loving. Liaisons between the younger man and the older married woman are likely to happen more often because the women stay more attractive and there are more of them available, because more women with successful marriages feel freer to face the challenges of an affair, and because age differences make these liaisons more interesting, not less, as sex becomes explored for its own sake and is more widely understood.

Beyond these general sociological considerations, however, it is also worth discussing why a particular stable and outwardly successful marriage that has endured for so long might still harbor a secret affair, when others would not. The "search for a son–mother relationship" was not, according to Jo, significant in her case. What then was the set of individual reasons that motivated her, in this and in the second affair? Jo wrote:

> Writing about my first extra-marital affair has made me think quite deeply about my past life, and I now realize that there are some aspects of this that had definite effects on future behavior for long or short periods, and I would like to expand on some of these.
>
> As a teenager, I was a flirt, and I still am, for that matter. In other words, I enjoyed the verbal sexual encounters with the opposite sex that went no further than this. I have always liked men, and enjoyed their company, but I am equally happy to make friends with women, and have some very good friends of my own sex.
>
> I started having sex long before my marriage, and there were several men before I met him. I never established what I considered a satisfactory relationship, however, and cannot remember ever having any feelings about sex that were different from the common one for girls: "Is this what it's all about? I wonder why such a big deal is made about it." No bells rang or anything like that, and I, like many women, never achieved an orgasm. When I met the man who is now my husband, we avoided pre-marital sex. We waited for years before we had sex, and then it was on our wedding night, and just as much of a disappointment for me as sex had ever been. However, it did not remain so for long. We loved each other, and there was a high level of sexual attraction between us, and I learned quite quickly just what a full sexual relationship meant. I made the

vow of faithfulness to myself because I knew myself sufficiently well to know that I was still likely to be attracted by other attractive men. In other words, I deliberately switched off completely as far as other men were concerned.

It was the fact that I only found a satisfactory sexual relationship in marriage that made me question the wisdom of pre-marital sex, and I still question it. I cannot be alone in this, for there must be many girls who need the security of love and a settled situation to grow sexually. The ultimate in communication between the sexes cannot take place as part of a clandestine affair, full of worry and doubt and fear. I certainly need that security, and yet I have to accept the logic that tells me that I am illicitly in love, with no security about my lover except the utter certainty that he loves me as much as I love him. I am tempted to come to the conclusion that women are illogical creatures, and that I am truly feminine to be so inconsistent, but there has to be an answer in my own psyche. I think it is this: that pre-marital sex was a great disappointment and a peril, that my marriage helped me understand my sexuality and to have a fulfilling and rewarding life, and that even so my marriage has had many, many bitter moments of loneliness and anger. With my lover I reap the benefit of being sexually alive in every way; with my early past now firmly in its place I can love without the same fear, knowing what it all means.

Jo can hardly reproach herself for the marriage, and she sees the particular advantages of an affair later in life, now that she has atoned for earlier "mistakes." Yet, like so many who have affairs, she seems to be more alive because she is truer to herself, to the sexually adventurous, flirtatious little girl, set aside years ago and for many years forgotten, while she spent her time trying to be the person she thought she should be, not the person she was. She still has the talent she exercised recklessly in her youth, and now she can exercise it again, more securely.

The cliché of the middle-aged family man smitten with his flirtatious young secretary at the office is a common one of television scripts. Cliché or not, it is in fact a frequent occurrence. The older man who is sexually attracted to a younger woman knows only too well the risk he runs of looking foolish. Nonetheless, older men do often yearn for the youth they squandered, and older women truly feel that their beauty could not hold a man enraptured these days as once it did. They have had fantasies of such affairs, and many of those who laugh loudest at the TV cliché have had more than fantasies. Most wives understand this vulnerability, and in a good marriage they can usually share the anxiety of it, and end with a reassuring laugh about the whole thing. Women who, at an early age, fall in love with older married men are like women of any age who fall in love—full of doubts and hesitancies, not willing to get more involved sexually than they are able to handle emotionally, cautious and often very frightened. The irony that is seldom explored by the cliché is how like the wives they are, how often equally conforming. This too could easily be dramatized out of all proportion, but it is seldom noticed. Ordinary families absorb the problem because so often the characters concerned let it evaporate by avoiding melodrama.

Where a marriage is insecure and the older man has affairs with other women, the women are just as likely to be older as younger. Perhaps one reason why the stereotype has such popularity, however, is that younger women can seem more of a threat. Jo describes her feelings:

> I doubt if my husband would choose a young girl to have an affair with, but I suppose he might, and there the physical appearance might cause some doubt or jealousy. Surely I have much more to offer him in so many other ways, and he does not appear in any way to have tired of my body. Perhaps I am used to his being among young girls and women in any case, because of his work, yet I've never worried about this. If he did, perhaps I would rather not know. I don't think I would feel particularly threatened.

Yet to many wives with adolescent families it is not the contrast between their aging body and that of the young girl, still beautiful in the traditional way, that alone constitutes the threat. It is also the fact that the younger woman can have babies, and, if her husband leaves her for a younger woman, the thought of his fathering a new brood must be especially threatening. In Jo's case her husband's vasectomy would prevent this. The fact that male sterilization when a family is complete means a man will not have a family with another woman may well increase its popularity with some wives.

If she does feel threatened by a much younger woman, a middle-aged wife can often act with a speed and ruthlessness that surprises even herself.

"As soon as I found out," one interviewee said, "I got her name and phone number and called her from the lawyer's office. I said either she left him alone or there would be a divorce, and her parents would be informed she had broken up my marriage." Liz, whose affair with one of her professors, a man of forty-eight, was referred to earlier, had a similar experience.

When his wife found out she ranted and raved and shouted and got every single detail out of him, then packed a suitcase. She said he could choose right then and there, and if he chose me that's the last he'd see of her. He called me and told me with her in the room with him, and I was heartbroken. I did not want to break up his marriage and neither did he. I saw him once more on his own later, and he told me she had said she could not have done it if she hadn't lost control.

Sometimes the younger woman is not discovered, and then she may well dedicate her life to her otherwise-married man and become in effect a second, part-time wife. The large age difference often means that the man can afford to keep her while she has a baby, and this happened to one interviewee, Maureen. She lives in an apartment, is thirty-five, and has an eighteen-month-old baby. Her man is fifty, and she says she is not sexually interested in anyone else.

It began nearly eight years ago. We worked together, the usual office romance, you might say. He encouraged me, and helped me develop my talents. Now my earning power is even more than his, as a matter of fact. His wife was very understanding at first. We met at a party. She said she preferred their marriage to be basically a friendship, and actually encouraged an affair. My own situation was that during those first two years I wanted more than anything to have his child. There were several tries on my part. In the end I went to a specialist, and so did he, and he was fertile but I wasn't, so I had an operation. The ins and outs of those years, I won't go into. They were sheer hell at times.

Anyway, I got pregnant, and then I thought we would be together. But she changed her mind again and enticed him back. I had to do it all alone. It was not an easy birth, and there were difficulties about carrying the baby near to term, as I had a weak cervix or something. We got through it, though. He couldn't be with me, and he never saw the baby until a week after I got home with him. I don't think my daughter will suffer, but I'd like another baby, and it has to be his. He's the only man in my life. It doesn't look likely, however. She's still got him under her not inconsiderable thumb.

The baby is looked after during the day by a capable nurse, and she has returned to work as a high-powered executive.

Where I work they are very understanding, although there were a few eyebrows raised at first when I used to come in all swollen and looking contented. I think I'm quite a good mother, and, yes, I do think of myself as a wife. He and his little daughter get on very well. She's a sweet child; she makes friends with everyone. It seems as though there isn't any real future in it, although I would like him by my side all the time. We're none of us getting any younger, and when she [the baby] gets married he'll be over seventy. His own son married two years ago, and his wife [the son's] is pregnant now, he says. So I'm stuck with a grandfather for a lover, I tell him. I get bitter sometimes, but it was my doing as much as his, and my baby has a right to grow up without bitterness. She doesn't miss him yet, but I expect when she gets used to other kids who know their daddies she might.

I don't really know if he's told his wife everything about me. He says he gave her the impression once that we'd broken up, and that was soon after I knew I was going to have the baby. We don't discuss her or his marriage much. I like to take the pressure off him, and that would increase it. It's not her I'm really concerned about. She needn't feel threatened by me.

We're happy enough this way, and she's got him most of the time.

It is, perhaps, not strange that affairs with a large age difference should be regarded more as a source of dramatics when the man is an older, married partner, rather than when the woman is. The older married man with a young unmarried mistress can step more easily into a new and fertile marriage than can an older married woman with a young unmarried man. The older woman tends to be accepted socially as lessening in her beauty. The older man is often seen as more attractive with age, and, since many more of the stereotype dramas are written by men than by women, perhaps a sexist fantasy is at the heart of the matter. Furthermore, when an older woman has an affair of this kind, it is less likely to produce hysterics from the man, partly because he can take it as *carte blanche* to go and do likewise. When the shoe is on the other foot, the older wife is less likely to feel able to achieve a tit-for-tat conquest— certainly she is less likely to think she can find someone. As Jo argues:

Men's bodies, if they look after themselves, do not seem to age in the same way as women's; they haven't had them swollen and used by having babies. This doesn't mean I disliked being pregnant—I enjoyed all but the last tedious month, but had an easy labor and delivery and adored my baby—but it does mean that all the dieting and exercise in the world cannot restore that virginal shape. This may be one of the reasons why one hears more often about older-men–young-girl relationships rather than the other way around. Older men often have a sophistication that young men do not.

CHAPTER TEN

The morality of affairs

THERE ARE CURRENTLY MORE THAN 2,240,000 MARRIAGES every year—
2,284,000 in 1973 and 2,243,000 in 1978. Divorces are being made
absolute at a rate in excess of 1,100,000 a year—915,000 in 1973 but
1,122,000 in 1978, and an average each year since 1975 of 1,083,000.
Divorce petitions and final divorces have increased steadily. During
the last seven years, the number of marriages has tended to fall,
although 1978 saw an increase from the previous year.

Many factors affect the rates of marriage and divorce: changes
in the proportion of the population of marriageable age, changes in
the law on divorce that might make divorce easier or more difficult,
general economic trends, and a host of sociological factors to do
with attitudes toward both marriage and divorce. Of course there is
no connection between the number of marriages in a single year
and the number of divorces, because the people who are marrying
are not the same people who are divorcing. Nevertheless it keeps
matters in proportion to recognize that there are currently one-third
as many divorces each year as there are marriages, and at least one

in three women can expect to be divorced at least once before she reaches the age of forty-five.

It is not possible to count the number of affairs, although many divorces are finalized on the grounds of adultery. It seems reasonable to assume that adultery takes place in many more than just these marriages, and that it is not often cited as the main reason for the divorce petition. Consequently, it would be very surprising if there were not far more extra-marital affairs each year than there were divorces. There are approximately 100 million married people in the United States, roughly half of whom are under forty-five years old. If two out of every hundred of them have only one affair each year, this will exceed the combined total of marriages and divorces. Such a low figure as two percent would probably be an underestimate in most people's experience.

There can be no doubt that the lives of a very large proportion of married men and women are being enriched and made more meaningful by secret sexual relationships. Husbands and wives who think of their marital partner as happy and faithful are often, in fact, benefiting from something of which they know nothing, and which, if they knew, might destroy their peace of mind for a long time to come. The spouse they think of as normal, respectable, calm and capable, tender and gentle in bed, dedicated and exclusively theirs, is in fact able to remain so only because he or she is passionate and guilty, in love and abandoned to illicit sexual pleasure, a tiger in someone else's bed, a baby in the arms of a secret lover. Some of these affairs may surface one day, and explode into the life of the unsuspecting partner. The marriage will be over, and a new marriage may begin. Most will probably never be revealed or discovered, and may remain the most significant event in the life of the adulterous partner, a source of far more love and emotional growth than ever stemmed from the undisturbed, "perfect," and "successful" marriage.

People have affairs because it is through love and through sex that we grow, and because their marriages are not adequate to sustain a lifetime of constant emotional growth. There are two kinds of affairs: those that help people make sense of their need to grow from adolescence into fully sexual adults, and those that help people into their middle years as fully developed loving adults. Both types of affair—the "adolescent" and the "middlescent" affair—have common factors. They also have differences.

The common factors have to do with the need to feel wanted and loved in a new way, so that the loving sexual relationship that grows illicitly can use a part of the individual that is underdeveloped. Sexual curiosity can be exercised and satisifed. Skills can be improved and new confidence built. Sexual needs can be met more fully, and different kinds of orgasm experienced in different ways, so that the person concerned discovers a new and exciting range of ways in which his or her body can be aroused and fulfilled. People learn to value their bodies in a different context.

The differences have to do with why this is important to the individual concerned. Affairs that take place as a continuation of adolescence are a reaction to the old family politics, and to marriages that were contracted as a continuation of the complex power struggles of their parents. Such affairs are secret in the same way that adolescent sex explorations would have been secret. Similar feelings are experienced, the dramatic fallings in love, the consuming guilt, the same rebellious thrill, and the accumulating of points as a badge of achievement. The marital partner is not told because of the same mixture of feelings that would have applied—or did apply—to parents. They would feel let down, shocked, angry, and hurt. Their image of the good child they had shared so much with, sacrificed so much for, would be shattered. Not telling preserves the freedom of the adolescent to go on experimenting and searching until an objective is reached and the results can be made official: A new spouse has been found, and a new family can be planned and conceived. The new couple are in love. At last each has found his predestined mate, and they have grown out of the restricted family circle of parental possession of which their marriage is just an extension. So a former partner is abandoned and a fresh start is made.

The affair of "middlescence" comes to those whose adolescence is complete. They know their bodies well as old friends, and have a developing sense of the need for a life purpose beyond alternate acts of sex and love, work and leisure. To the middlescent, adult life appears acceptable but lacks meaning. Too little of it is dedicated to complete achievement. Many of these people have become profit

centers, so to speak, in their spouse's corporation, departments of
another life, not companies in their own right. They long to feel
wanted and purposeful, giving and complete for themselves. It
would be easy to plod along in a half-life. They choose to risk
disaster to gain a fuller, more meaningful use of their integrated
abilities as whole adults. Husbands, wives, children, work, and
friends split them into compartments. In middlescent years an affair
makes them whole, and they can grow again.

The idea of marriage and the experience of an extra-marital
affair are incompatible. An affair is a contradiction of marriage. It
is simply not possible for most people to so dedicate their emotional
growth to one exclusive relationship to the extent that this relationship is not damaged by an affair. Most people in our society feel too
threatened to enable their partners to achieve emotional growth
through sex with a third party. The myths of marriage help to
perpetuate emotional immaturity. Parents deliberately prevent their
children from achieving more freedom than they could handle
themselves. They see merit in this restriction, since they are themselves afraid of sex and of freedom, and particularly of sexual
freedom. The institution of marriage is too often not only a defense
against unbridled sexuality; it is also a defense against emotional
growth.

But for millions of people, the officially approved methods of
making sense of life through marriage do not work. Their choice is
a stark one. Something is missing from their lives. They have been
encouraged to expect less than fulfillment and to accept this and
carry on as less than complete people. They have accepted the bribes
of marriage: comfort, status, permission to have children, the approval of parents and colleagues. Many of them have been loud in
the justification of the bribe system. Then they meet somebody else,
and have to face up to the fact that something is still missing. Life
suddenly has a new meaning for them, but to follow a new course
will mean a rejection of the marriage, and a deliberate wrecking of
somebody else's comfortable dependency upon them. Do they hurt
the people whom they love a great deal in order to risk success or
failure with someone they know less but love more? The whole
system will be against them. The bribes will be withdrawn. The
stark choice is between selfishness, which they know they need,

and self-sacrifice, which will ultimately destroy them. So millions compromise. They and their affairs develop in secret. They learn new ways to love and be loved, but their one official partner with whom they vowed to share all their most significant experiences is never told.

People have affairs because the institution of marriage as it is officially recognized simply does not work. It can fail in two ways. First, it does not provide anything like the ideal basis for raising children that it is claimed to provide. Children are the products of the relationship between their parents not just in the sense that they are conceived through a sexual act, but also in the sense that they themselves are profoundly influenced in the course of their childhood by the nature of the relationship between their parents. Most parents are themselves incomplete adults. Their marital relationships reflect this. They pass on to their children their own uncertainties about each other, about their own bodies, about sex and pleasure. Day after day, as their children grow, all the sexual conflicts that pass unresolved between the parents are communicated through the children, and are built into their personalities. The fears of the parents become the self-control systems of their children. When a child is punished or frightened by a parent for the child's own good, the fiercest punishment is reserved for those behaviors that frighten the parents most. The child learns not to frighten the parent, and controls its own behavior to this end. Only when it is big enough not to be frightened can the grown-up child review the systems of self-control that it learned in childhood. This process of review forms the central feature of adolescence. Most people in contemporary society never complete the review before they, in their turn, become parents.

One reason marriage can fail, therefore, is that parents use children to avoid coming to terms with their hang-ups, to avoid sorting themselves out, and so pass their problems on to their children instead. Then they pressure their children into getting married. When the children get married, they (the parents) expect it to be to people of whom they approve—people, that is, with similar hang-ups. The result is a new family unit with unresolved conflicts very like their own. However, should this new unit show any signs of real independence, or of resolving this legacy of conflict by renouncing the marriage, then both partners are branded as "failures," and the marriage is called a "broken" marriage. No blame is attached to the parents.

Second, marriage fails because it is designed to prevent people's gaining a wide variety of sexual and loving experience. It is based on the renunciation of unrestricted emotional growth. The vows that people take on their wedding day, when traditionally both are supposed to be virgins, are that neither partner, for the rest of his and her life, will ever make love with somebody else. Any possibility that they might be wrong for each other is ruled out by this. The chance that each might change is not envisioned. Should one of them change, and be driven by the need for a new understanding of sex and love to express this in an affair, while the other remains stuck at the same stage of emotional growth, then the blame falls on the one who grows, while the one who remains stagnant is seen as "innocent" and "wronged."

We live in a society in which marriage and family are loudly proclaimed as our finest achievements. More of us are getting married than ever before. More of us are getting married more than once. Yet the claims we make as a society are utterly at variance with the personal experience of millions of individuals. Officially we are a monogamous society. Unofficially we are polygamous. Officially our marriages are havens of peace where we share our deepest joys. Unofficially they are frequently economic arrangements based on unattainable ideals of honesty wherein we spin a web of deceit to hide our deepest joys and protect our moments of true peace. Officially we grow to maturity by limiting our sexual experience to one official partner. Unofficially we recognize that this would keep us immature, and that true maturity more often comes from a wider experience of sex and love with unofficial partners. Officially we exercise self-control, that mysterious psychological process whereby we prevent ourselves from doing what we feel like doing because it might threaten those principles we learned from our parents. Unofficially we abandon self-control, and grow through those barriers of pain and guilt that our parents could not face. Officially marriage works for the vast majority. Unofficially it works for far fewer people—those whose marriages are an expression of full maturity, and those whose immaturity rests undisturbed on total conformity to parental control.

It will no doubt be argued, loudly in some quarters, that all this is grossly immoral. There is an old-fashioned name for extra-marital sex. It is called *adultery*. To commit adultery is to break the seventh commandment, and thus to sin against the oldest and most respected moral code still regarded as valid by our civilization. Adultery is still regarded as evidence of the irretrievable breakdown of marriage. It leads to lies and deceit, to betrayal of trust, and to unhappiness. To the old-fashioned moralist it is indecent and sinful to present extra-marital sex as anything beneficial to the individuals concerned, and an act of gross moral turpitude to encourage married people to become adulterers. Some of these moralists rest their case on a literal adherence to the injunctions of the *Bible*. Those who do so will seek in vain an appropriate punishment for adulterers. The Book of Exodus lists penalties for breaking the other command-ments—for example, "he that curseth his father or his mother shall surely be put to death" (Exodus 21:17). It lists no penalty for adultery, and there are precedents for rejecting stoning to death as the answer.

Not all moral opponents of adultery argue from a fundamen-talist view of the *Bible*. In general, there are three main arguments against adultery. The first is that it is immoral because marriage is an ideal to be strived for, at which many will fail, but that all should struggle to attain; in regarding adultery as immoral, many more people are helped than are hurt. People, it is argued, need to have an ideal they can attempt to reach, and sexual exclusivity, if it can be achieved, ennobles the individual and leads to wisdom and peace of mind. It is recognized that many will fail, and the charity of the morally pure should not be withheld when such erring souls cry out for comfort. From this moral stance, emotional growth resulting from adultery is false growth. True growth comes from self-sacrifice. The duty of such moralists toward adulterers is to help them understand the virtues of self-sacrifice, and to prevent immoral people from gaining rewards of any sort as a result of their behavior.

The second main moral argument against adultery is that it is essentially selfish. The adulterer gains emotional satisfaction by exploiting through deceit the "innocent" partner. For example, when a husband has an affair, this is sometimes made possible because his wife continues to provide a home, to cook and wash, to look after the children, and to support him emotionally while he goes off and gets his growth at the cost of hers. Or, if the wife is secretly adulterous, it is the husband who is exploited, especially if he earns the money she spends on her lover, and looks after the children while she is in bed with another man. Whether one or both partners have a secret affair, to do so is to rob the other of time they could spend together to make their relationship work. They belittle each other through this exploitation. The fact that an adulterous spouse says nothing of the adultery to the other partner is also morally wrong because it so often reflects a patronizing attitude in the marriage, an assumption that one can handle emotional growth only if the other remains static. The sexist double standard—both male and female chauvinism—is often based on such exploitations of emotional deprivation.

The third of these moral aruguments against extra-marital sexual adventures takes the form of a defense of marriage on the grounds that, for all its faults, there is nothing better to put in its place. Marriage, it is argued, is essential for a great many men and women because without the full security of knowing that they are important enough to their partner to merit the compliment of monogamy, they will never fully develop sexually and emotionally. Women, for example, need to know that for the rest of their lives they are the only mate their husband will make love to. This is an emotional need, and one that has sexual consequences. It enables a woman to give herself completely to a man, and only through this timeless giving, it is maintained, can she learn slowly and thoroughly the full sexual flowering of her own body, through orgasm and child-birth to motherhood and full maturity. She and her one life-partner must learn this together, knowing each other's ways, so that when things are not perfect they both have the security to benefit mutually from their mistakes, and to grow together. If they did not have this security, each would turn to other partners, and have to start again from the beginning. Neither of them would ever grow past the mistakes they made together.

This is not a sexist view, either, for men also need a long-term, stable, "giving" relationship to reach full sexual maturity. If a man knows that this one woman will always love him exclusively, it is argued, he can learn, little by little, how to express the full range of his sexuality, from virility to being the little boy, through the conscious achievement of her orgasm to unconscious and effortless arousal and simultaneous orgasm, and so through mutual loving to responsible and joyful fatherhood. Long-term stability in a relationship is seen as essential to emotional development, and only marriage, it is claimed, provides a strong enough framework to guarantee this. The question is a moral one in that each individual is morally entitled to such growth, and in reaffirming the moral rightness of marriage—and the immorality of anything that destroys it—society is upholding an essential right of all the individuals who make it up. Such moralists recognize that a large number of married people do not achieve their full growth potential through marriage.

Against these three moral arguments can be set two counter-claims. The first is that marriage often seems to do more harm than good. The second is that it is not a moral issue at all, and that in discussing marriage and adultery the moralists have no justifiable claim to special pleading.

On the first issue—that marriage does more harm than good—there can be no doubt that several million people in our society are engaged in secret affairs in order to counterbalance in their own lives the effects of deprivation and emotional stagnation that their full adherence to the ideals of marriage would perpetuate or worsen. People are suffering because their marriages are not working, and because they dare not or will not find extra-marital lovers. Their children also suffer, since the unresolved conflicts inside such marriages inevitably influence their children's future behavior. Our unconscious behavior is not a mysterious expression of deeply hidden animal desires; it is the emergence in adult behavior of responses to emotional stress—positive and negative—that we learned in childhood when others older than we had the power to control the outcome of our behavior.

However, it can hardly be said yet that marriage does more harm than good. A quantitative assessment of this kind is beyond us. Nobody knows how many marriages lead to affairs, nor what gain or loss results from adultery, or from the rejection of adultery as a solution to the strains of married life. But it is true that the traditional ideal of marriage has failed to live up to its promise for many millions of people. Therefore there should be a wider and more sensitive awareness at large of the ways people build false hopes of marriage, the dangers of these unrealistic expectations, and the ways they can be helped through crisis to emotional, social, and intellectual fulfillment, with or without marriage.

What, then, is the answer to the moral problems posed by the extra-marital affair? The first step is to recognize that not every "problem" has to have a "solution." Perhaps we are too prone to seeing every issue as requiring an answer, part of the unfortunate consequence of our fascination for sociology at the cost of our understanding of psychology. Every individual works out personal ways of coming to terms with reality. In so doing some ask for help and some do not. A healthy society will be equipped to answer the former and not to impede the latter. By such means, little by little, things change.

Today, marriages of the conventional kind are less and less likely. Fewer parents expect their children to be virgins at marriage. More are likely to remain concerned with the quality of the marriage, and to help the partners through those early years when separation is more common and admitting failure is harder. Yet most parents dread the thought that their teenage son or daughter will have an affair with a married person. Most face with anger and fear the news that their married child is adulterous. As a society we still have to face up to the part played in our emotional growth by sex with loving strangers, inside and outside marriage. We still expect people to be grateful for our own self-sacrifice, even when they were damaged by it.

If the first step is to recognize that there need not be a solution, is there a second step? There should be solutions for those who cannot find one for themselves without some guidance from other people. We are all, in some way, victims of social attitudes toward adultery. Many unmarried people live incomplete, unfulfilled lives because of the burden of the high ideals of marriage. They cannot make relationships that meet these ideals, and they have nowhere to turn in order to rebuild their lives in a less idealistic way. They form one sad segment of the lonely cohorts of our society. Too little is done for them, to help them know themselves, meet others, and learn new skills. Many are shy. All are easily exploited by computer-dating agencies and expensive "friendship clubs" designed to help them fill in time and not grow. There is no legal requirement for any of these organizations to employ fully qualified, independent counselors.

Some unmarried people lead sad, lonely, unfulfilled lives because they are in love with married people who cannot or will not marry them. This is often a phase of emotional growth that concludes with the end of the affair. Often the affair never ends, and the sacrifice is of the family they never had. As a society we reject with moral fervor the unmarried woman who has a baby by her married lover. She may be regarded, for example, as unfit to teach children. She is often better off if nobody knows who the father is, and to plan to have a baby is thought of as more evil than to get caught accidentally and to keep the child.

Many married people, actively engaged in secret affairs, are torn apart by needless guilt, because help and guidance are not available except from the worthy moralist or the unqualified amateur. Marriage guidance is changing, but it is still largely seen as a way of preserving marriages at the cost of emotional damage and potential growth. Conciliation services to help divorcing couples are slowly being introduced. Many people are hurt by their marriage because they refuse to have affairs. They cannot ask for help, either. There is simply nowhere for them to go. Their frustration eats away at all their relationships, with children and with spouse, setting up a new generation of unhappy people.

As for the future, it is to be hoped that the most damaging expectations of marriage will disappear of their own accord. Perhaps this is a vain hope. Until we have a society that values the mental health of its citizens as much as our own society values physical health, it is unlikely that marriage will be seen merely as one stage in the healthy development of an individual, and the extra-marital affair as an honest attempt to achieve more growth. Until then the issue will still be seen by many as one of morals, and those who, against the odds, dare to follow their feelings and break the rules will be forced to do so in secret, or risk the indignant wrath of those to whom immaturity is a badge to be worn with pride.

CHAPTER ELEVEN

The realities of affairs

WHATEVER THE MORALITY OF EXTRA-MARITAL AFFAIRS, and whatever the true number that take place each year, it is fair to say that a large number of people are affected by marital infidelity, either as active participants or as the spouse of one. In many cases it is a traumatic business—often needlessly so, in the opinion of many who have had affairs and of many who have not but are married to people who have. As a society we are committed to marriage, and often ambivalent toward infidelity. Yet once an affair has started, and we find ourselves faced with a distraught friend, few of us moralize about it. The priority has to be to offer practical help and guidance, and to accept the facts, in much the same way that, although many nurses and doctors may privately condemn pre-marital sex, they help those people who are in trouble over it. As a result, the single population can receive excellent guidance on how to have sex successfully without being married. None of this guidance seems to tell them what to do if their partner is married. Nor is there any guidance for the married person who is having an affair with another married person. The view seems to be that this might merely encourage it—a view that is unfortunately only too familiar in another guise to those who help the unmarried to understand sex.

The fact must be faced that a significant proportion of married people will have affairs, and that many of them feel the need for help in avoiding failure—the failure that results in other people's being hurt very badly. It is too late to tell them now that they should not have started in the first place. What, then, are the general rules for achieving a successful extra-marital affair? It is a question that three categories of people will wish to consider: the married person having an affair, the single lover, and the spouse of the married person concerned. Of course, not all lovers in this sense are single, but those who are still married are included in the first category.

The married person
having an affair

If you are married, and you are having an affair, you might fit any of the categories so far mentioned in this book: You may be having one affair, or more than one; you may regard it as primarily a love affair, or as mainly a matter of sex; your partner in the affair may be of your own age group, or may be much older or younger than you; and you may be having an affair with somebody who is single, or somebody who is still actively married to somebody else. Some of the following notes will apply to you whichever category you are in—and you may be in several.

The first thing to do if you have decided to have a successful affair is to be clear as to what you want to achieve. This is true of almost everything, but where affairs are concerned it is often especially difficult. The reason for this is that most people who have affairs are motivated to a greater or lesser extent by a need to meet unconscious objectives—that is, to try exploring a part of themselves that they cannot see clearly or be rational about. An affair is not something that feels logical or reasoned. Often what you want to achieve is not something you can express in cold, calculated words. Instead it is a feeling that is hard to define. A great many people who have affairs seem to be searching for a feeling or set of feelings that they have a need to experience, and that they themselves are still testing out and exploring through the affair itself.

If this is true in your case, it may help to try to list the feelings that predominate in your affair. Some will be feelings you like, and some you dislike. For example, you may value the feeling of loving and being loved, but hate the guilt and fear, jealousy and separation. The excitement of going to see your lover may be important, or there may not be any particular thrill in this. You may feel a staggering emotional completeness when the two of you are together, or perhaps a relaxed, peaceful sense of belonging. It may be the escape that matters, so that once free of your own home and on the way to your lover's home you feel relief and a sense of freedom. Or the worry and anxiety of being split between the two roles of lover and spouse could be paramount. Whatever you actually feel, good or bad, it helps to work out how much time you spent last week feeling all the different emotional states you go through. Try to be honest about time. Two hours spent in dread for the sake of the half an hour that makes up for them are still two hours of dread and half an hour of bliss. Add up the positives and the negatives into an audit of your feelings.

In general, people spend most time in any activity acquiring the feelings that they need the most. They often deny this, but it is still true. For example, a compulsive gambler spends most of his time losing, but denies that this is why he gambles. He says that he does it to win. Yet his conscious motivation to win is usually very much weaker than his unconscious motivation to lose. In the same way, an alcoholic spends more time being miserable and expressing remorse and shame than he (or she) spends being drunk and happy. Yet alcoholics often deny the unconscious motive—a need to feel degraded and a craving for forgiveness—and often stress the conscious motive, the one they spend least time on: that is to say, being happy.

In the same way, people who have affairs often deny that they have a need for the negative feelings that go with them—doubt, shame, guilt, fear, anger. They tend instead to stress the positive, conscious reasons for their behavior—love, tenderness, excitement, belonging, sexual pleasure, delight, and so on. Both sets of feelings, the positive and the negative, are normal—having an affair is not evidence of emotional illness, like compulsive gambling or alcoholism! It is normal to deny one's need for the negative, however, and to regard such feelings as something you wish to avoid but have to go through to get the better, positive feelings. In this way we reject our unconscious motivation. If you are going to have a successful affair, you cannot afford to reject these possible unconscious objectives out of hand. Only if you try to understand your need to feel negative as well as positive emotional states will your motivation become clearer to you. If, when you are strictly honest, you find that you are spending more time experiencing negative feelings rather than positive, pleasant ones, then your main needs may have to do with this, and not with the more obvious rewards that the affair brings. If the reverse is true—really true—then you are married in name only, and you might just as well be unmarried as married. You will not be seeking advice, either because you are quite remarkably well matched in marriage, or because you are far too self-centered to recognize the difference between a successful affair and a disaster.

It is more likely that you experience pretty well the same amount of time in bad feelings as in good ones, and that it is difficult to decide which predominates. Whatever your audit shows, however, here is a possible next step.

First, try to work out where it was you learned to need those negative feelings—for example, fear of discovery. This may have been a very important part of your adolescence, because at that time in your life you felt that you had to conceal from parents the true extent of your sexual experience. Maybe you hid for years the fact that you were not a virgin, or the fact that you masturbated. Both these secrets are of the reassuringly normal kind, but it will help you to understand your own objectives if you consider whether or not you are now using your spouse as a stand-in for your parents, and doing a little private catching up on unfinished adolescent development. You may have had to restrict the amount of sexual exploration you could undertake in adolescence—fear of unwanted pregnancies, the pressure to complete your education, responsibilities at home that forced you to neglect opportunities for meeting the opposite sex, and many other reasons may have been responsible. Or perhaps you wanted to fall in love and never did, or to feel the thrill of sexual ecstasy but were disappointed. Whatever your reason for trying to catch up on missed adolescent development, your parents' attitudes at the time will have been a very powerful force in your life. If you are now using your spouse as a stand-in parent, you may make the mistake of expecting your spouse to behave exactly as your parents would have acted. Those people who learn in adolescence that good experiences are inaccessible without negative feelings (like fear of discovery) often learn to need negative feelings in order to achieve positive ones. In your adolescence, your parents, whatever their faults, gave you the security of something to rebel against. If you later have affairs with the spouse as a stand-in parent, your prime need is to protect that security. Fear of discovery is an unconscious expression of the need for security, in the sense that a child needs to know that its parents will always be there. In an affair where this feeling predominates, you can gain most from helping your spouse feel secure in positive ways. You can use new sexual experience positively with your spouse, to give reassurance and pleasure, and to show your love as having real continuity in your life together. If you can, tell your lover that this is what you are doing.

You may have learned to expect negative feelings as part of a love experience much earlier than adolescence. A sense of guilt is often part of the fear of discovery. This can happen because of a need in childhood to please one parent in some ways, and the other parent in quite different ways. Mothers indulge some children, saying, "Don't tell your father"—and vice versa. This can result in a situation where the child does not really know how to please either parent without lying and feeling guilty about it. Your present feelings of guilt may be of this kind, so that you are not sure how to lie without ever feeling guilty. If you have a tendency to feel a lot of guilt, beware of bullying your spouse or lover, of having tantrums and long bad moods. You have simply set yourself up to try to please two different "parent" figures, your spouse and your lover, so that you can play one off against the other. Take the pressure off both of them by arguing less, allowing the last word to them when you need it most. Neither is your parent, and unlike your parents they have the right to reject you and may exercise that right. So, if you want a successful affair, it is best not to stir up trouble with one and then go to the other for consolation.

A sense of guilt can also come from an excessive need to conform to a set of ideals that your extra-marital affair proves you cannot live up to. A possible cause of this is that you had one weak parent and one very strong parent. The simplest explanation is that you take after both, the weak one failing and the strong one setting the ideals. Again, this is normal behavior, and it becomes neurotic only when people repeat, time after time, such obvious failures that they are constantly humbling themselves and asking for forgiveness. Beware, however, of unconsciously trying to achieve failure, even if nobody ever knows, and you never ask for forgiveness. You may deceive yourself that your affair *and* your marriage are both brilliant successes, only to find one day that you are sounding just like the parent you most dislike. A successful affair in your case is one where you learn to be like neither parent, but a person in your own right.

If you are lucky, and you are aware of unconscious objectives as well as conscious ones, then you can not only begin to accept the mixture but also strengthen all your relationships by using your personality to develop a much deeper sensitivity to the way other people feel. This is the great advantage of a successful affair: your getting to know yourself better and using it to become more sensitive and loving all around. Affairs for sex only can do this if they stop your putting sexual pressure on a spouse who does not want it, but they have the major disadvantage that you are not likely to feel more loved or to become more lovable, and your spouse's dislike of sex becomes more, not less, of a problem, since you become less willing to be loving and patient with the spouse as time goes by. Sex-by-proxy affairs are often connived at by spouses who "don't want to be told if you ever have an affair." The spouse, in other words, wants a quiet life sexually, and unless there is solid companionship in an elderly marriage in which sex has faded naturally into an annual event, the reasons for this should never be left uninvestigated. A spouse who connives at a sex-by-proxy affair is often playing a solo power game, with the other spouse as the victim. The best answer is to drop the affair and to examine the possibilities for rescuing the marriage. If this is impossible, use affairs to find a real partner who loves you, and then the two of you have to face the problem together and do the best to find a solution you can both accept.

All this applies much more clearly to the married person having one affair than to those involved in multiple affairs. Keeping several affairs going at once requires not only very special organizational talent, but also a rather unusual motivation. If you are involved in more than two affairs, then there is a special need to ask yourself why. This is because the risks involved are so much higher. Not just the risk of being found out, but also the risk to your spouse and lovers if only one of them contracts venereal disease. You may feel sure that this is not a real risk, but there is also the fact to be taken into account that you may well be perpetuating, rather than combatting, your own risk of failing to develop a better understanding of yourself. Why do you need to collect so many conquests? Why do you need so much of the same kind of love at the cost of developing a deeper relationship with one person? If the answer to this is that the lovers you have already are the wrong kind of people, then why are you not finding the right kind? Your actions show a deep need for reassurance, but it is clear also that you are an attractive person, well able to attract more compatible partners. You may well be wasting this ability in order to delay real maturity in response to some deeper, more unconscious motivation. Some people of this kind have an enormous capacity to go on loving and giving, to support emotionally several deeply intimate relationships simultaneously. They often have an underdeveloped capacity to receive love. Mature love takes as well as gives.

Of course, some multiple affairs involve very shallow relationships, and these selfishly use other people's capacity to love in order to satisfy one person's need for too much love of the wrong kind. The person at the center of multiple affairs is often very lonely, and the affairs can put off the day of reckoning when he or she comes to terms with the inner core of loneliness that lies at the center of true maturity. If this is you, then only you can face the loneliness inside you, and render it powerless to hurt you. This loneliness may well be founded in anger or a sense of injustice.

It is more than likely if you are having an affair with someone who has never been married that you often feel under pressure to divorce and marry your lover. This happens particularly with first affairs, when the two of you are least experienced in handling feelings of guilt and the extremes of passion and despair. The point to remember is that, however uncomfortable it is to suffer from doubt and guilt and despair, unless you know why these feelings hurt you, you will not be able to control them; and they will control you. The rush into another marriage to escape these feelings is merely to act out of negative feelings. Handling guilt is a matter not of denying the feeling but of sharing it, and trying to find out whose expectations of you you feel obliged to try unsuccessfully to meet. If you cannot discuss these feelings and explore them with your lover, there is a grave danger, should you both marry, of simply repeating the "mistakes" of your first marriage. Consider a few of the situations in which you feel most guilty, and see if any of them are "repeat performances" of past patterns.

Feeling guilty about not marrying your lover can come about as an internal way of paying for the good feelings—the love and the passion. The way this works is that many of us are trained in childhood to pay for our pleasures by knowing when to accept that enough is enough. For example, we are allowed to have our own way, to do what we like, but we are told sooner or later that we have gone far enough and must now knuckle under and accept discipline. Pleasure has to be paid for. To the child it seems that having your own way always ends in guilt. The childlike logic of this usually survives into adult life. So if we get a great deal more pleasure from an affair than we think we deserve, we expect to feel even more guilt.

In first affairs, the passions are deeper and more exciting simply because the affair is a replay of adolescent feelings—however old we are! The adolescent is extremely sensitive, and touches the depths of despair one moment and the heights of sublime passion the next. Idealism is often a large part of this—the need to do the right thing, and to feel guilty if it cannot be done. So first affairs often give far more guilt than they need—together with passions and depths of feelings that our friends smile about because they seem so disproportionate. The rebellious adolescent's constant cry is "they don't understand," and this is often the cry of the adult in a first affair—"they *wouldn't* understand." It is true. They wouldn't understand. The person you love like this seems quite the wrong type—so different, so apparently unlike your other friends. But then how often this is true of the exploratory, rebellious phase of late adolescence, when we try out as many possibilities as we can, and learn who suits us by failing to make lasting relationships with people who do not quite suit us! So it is far better to let things take their course in the affair, and give yourself time to gain new maturity from it, doing the least possible damage to everyone concerned until your new strength and self-awareness emerge. It goes without saying, of course, that you have an equal obligation to help your lover grow too, and your spouse.

There are a few other points worth making. Affairs that are for sex only seldom work for long: Once the courtship is over, they tend to collapse. Talking, in the long run, is much more important than sex. You will also have to be a good liar. If this is not a skill you already have, it is likely to develop. In effect, your lies to your spouse are designed to carve out an area of privacy, and to protect this from discovery. They are not designed to increase emotional dependence on you, yet this is often a side effect, simply because you have less time within the marriage to sort out the emotional issues that underlie economic dependence. Money, the children, the shopping, domestic arrangements of all sorts—these things are not simply matters of convenience and organization. They are also ways of showing that you care about your spouse. While you are having an affair, and developing your own identity somewhere else, it is only too easy to neglect the small domestic matters and let big emotional crises build up unnecessarily. If you love your spouse, say so, and show that you do. Give as much reassurance as you can, not out of guilt, nor in order to manipulate the situation, but genuinely. Loving two people (or more) is perfectly possible for most of us, and—if this is how you feel—then both the people you love should be able to feel assured of your love. To neglect one for the other is inevitable at times, but if you do this all the time you need to examine why you are doing so, or your capacity to create conflicts will remain greater than your ability to resolve them.

One school of thought suggests that the object of life is to be happy. This is countered by an opposite view that human beings are designed for problem solving, and that conflict is a normal part of life. Yet another view is that the objective of life is usefulness to other people. Whichever view you agree with, there is a high probability that part of your motivation in having an affair is to reassess where you are going, what you are doing with your "official" life, what life really means to you. These matters are too seldom discussed by adults. Nor, when they *are* discussed, do they get resolved. Some affairs help us avoid the issue. Other affairs help us confront it. The main thing is to know what you are doing, to accept in full the responsibility you have incurred by your actions, and to grow in responsibility, sensitivity, and creativity while you help others around you grow. If there is nobody in your life who knows the whole truth about your affairs, you are bound to feel lonely, and may well not know the whole truth yet about yourself.

The unmarried person having an affair

If you are single, you will fit into one of three categories: never married, divorced, or widowed or separated (and in effect divorced). The problems faced by each of these groups are different to some extent, and they also vary with age and experience. There are also some special difficulties faced by single men having affairs with married women that affect differently the partners in an affair between a married man and a single woman.

If you have never been married, then the first question most people will ask you is why not. They are more likely to ask this if you are over thirty than if you are younger. Many never-married people resent this, and know only too well the look in the eyes of the smugly married as they try to work out what is wrong with you. Perhaps you are still tied to parental apron strings, they think, or are sexually too timid, homosexual, or perverted. Or you may be seen as too selfish, content with the high disposable income that "singles" are thought to have, living the wild life, fancy-free and irresponsible. The "marriageable" age, between nineteen and twenty-four, may have passed you by without your meeting anyone you could marry, and the next five years may find you still unmarried. After this, the smug members of our marrying society begin to regard you as a special case, on the shelf as a permanent failure. The pressure increases. The more attractive you look, the more they try to keep their husband and wives from getting to know you, and the more they wish to believe that underneath you are some kind of psychiatric case, unable to relate to people.

The single girl who has an affair with a married man while she is still part of the nineteen-to-twenty-four age group faces several problems. First, she is under maximum pressure to marry: from society at large, from the fact that many of her contemporaries have married, and, above all, from her own parents. This may lead to several conflicts. She is likely to place undue pressure on her lover for him to leave his wife for her—undue because he is highly unlikely to do so, but very likely to feel that he ought to do so. The married man, moreover, is almost always jealous. He feels very insecure, and applies a double standard. He is allowed to love two people (his wife and his lover), but his lover is not. If she finds a second boyfriend to keep her going when her lover is not around— most of the time, in fact—he will be hurt and angry and physically jealous. The fact that she is part of the marrying-age group threatens him most of all. He feels doubly trapped, and resents his lover's freedom, though nevertheless benefiting from it at the same time. Because the young single girl can marry, but has not done so yet, she may well be coming to terms with her own and her parents' expectations with regard to marriage. Parents tend to disapprove totally of affairs with married men, and, if they are likely to misunderstand and not show any sympathy, they simply do not get told. So the girl may become trapped and isolated, unable to enjoy the feeling of status that public recognition of adult love should bring, unable to share her worries, and unable to find anyone else in place of her lover without risking hurting him deeply.

If you are trapped like this, examine the bars of your cage closely, and see why they are there. First, your parents. Their inability to understand is because they cannot yet accept your full right to be an independent grown-up with a sex life of your own, and because they will be disappointed in you and for you. Under-lying this is their own marital relationship together. Your actions draw attention to their failures, and give them an excuse to avoid solving their own problems, because they can worry about yours instead. Clearly it is time to make friends with at least one parent, and to start to share the joy and pain of being an adult. If only one parent can recognize that you understand how loving sex feels, he or she might be able to talk about his (or her) own problems on an equal level with you, as adult to adult, and the bars of the cage will be loosened. Some parents, for whatever reason, will not want to enter into this sort of intimacy with their children.

Second, your lover. The hurt he feels when he is jealous is the culmination of a long period of conditioning, and not simply all your fault. He needs to make sense of his own feelings, and the best offering you can give is comfort. Guilt will not help you to help him. If you can accept that he will not leave his wife and marry you, then this will help to keep the affair in proportion. Many married men having affairs exaggerate the extent to which sex does not work in their marriage. This is often a cry for reassurance, not an accurate statement of fact. So give the reassurance, but remember also that you are helping his marriage to work much more than you are helping your own relationship with him to last forever. If this is what you want to do, then to do it successfully you must work yourself out of a job sooner or later. Try to leave a lifelong friend behind when you do this—someone, somewhere, who will forever wish you well.

Third, you. The cage you are in is not just your inability to tell your parents, or to manage to live through the loneliness while your married lover is absent from you and you feel that you cannot start a new relationship. The cage is also your own body. When you are with your lover, this body has a clear value. It excites him, and you can feel that your body and the life you have are important. If other men do not attract you, this is because your lover brings to your body a very special value that does not exist without him. But it can also mean that you might have some negative personal feelings about your body that go away only when you are with him. Some women, for example, have deep-seated worries about their own attractiveness, that their breasts are too big or too small, that their face is not pretty, that their hair is all wrong, that they are too fat or too skinny. These fears are often without foundation, but it is important to try to make the best of your appearance.

The more mature single woman who has an affair with a married man may often be beautifully adjusted to it and feel quite happy that she is loved and cherished by him, except that she has very few of the advantages of being married, particularly those that go with official recognition. On the other hand, she may relish her unmarried freedom. As part of a long-term affair, she may well feel that she is really an unofficial wife, and it helps to have special common friends who accept the two people as a couple. One problem, however, against which there is practically no defense, is broodiness—and this can hit the man just as hard as the woman. Married couples who cannot have babies receive great public sympathy. The quasi-married woman, who has found the man she loves, but will not hurt him by forcing him to end his marriage, and cannot risk a pregnancy, gets no sympathy at all. There does not appear to be any defense against broodiness, but it can, if you are lucky in your man, be shared. This increases the pressure on him, but it is his pain too if he understands your pain, and sharing pain together is as important as sharing joy.

The unmarried man who has an affair with a married woman faces similar problems, except, perhaps, that he is under less pressure to become a married man. He too is called upon to provide solace and understanding while his lover unburdens herself of the pent-up frustrations of the marriage, and he may also feel trapped. Both have to come to terms with their own views and expectations of marriage, and with the fact that they provide support for their partner in another, more official, often more permanent relationship. Both also have to decide how much they want to know—all the intimate details of the life together of their partner and spouse tend to emerge, and the lover is often expected to take sides, and not to be dispassionate or balanced in his judgments. It probably helps to some extent if you know your lover's family—her husband, and her children if there are any. Yet this, too, is a trap. Knowing them means that you and your lover can spend more time together as part of the larger family group. But you cannot risk letting any of them know the true nature of the relationship unless you and your lover have decided that this is right. So it is not an easy matter to relax. It frequently rubs salt into the wound, increasing the hurt when you know them, but if you do not know them it is harder to understand your lover, and you feel more isolated when your lover is absent from you. Some affairs begin because you are already a friend of your lover's husband.

In trying to take stock of your situation, it is as well to face certain facts. If your lover's spouse finds out about your affair, you cannot expect kindness, love, and understanding, particularly at first, and even more so if you have been accepted by the person you have deceived as a friend and confidant. He or she will be deeply hurt, totally alone, and very angry. You will be despised and hated, probably pitied too. Some people say they do not care about this, others that their case is an exception. Unfortunately, no case is an exception, and everybody cares somewhere. You can avoid some of this by making sure that he or she never finds out, but the issue that should not be avoided, for your own sake, is why you are willing to risk this, and what made you into the person you are, willing and able to set yourself up as the victim of another person's jealous rage. Somewhere in the depths of your past you were raged at before. Is this a repeat performance of a significant family drama? If so, what can you learn about yourself that helps to explain what you are trying to do, and what does your lover see in you that enables him or her to risk a similar crisis?

The divorced
or widowed lover

If you are divorced or widowed, and you are having an affair with someone who is married, a great deal depends on the quality of your former married life. There are often periods of promiscuity in the first few years after a divorce, as the formerly married person tries to start again from the beginning, and to reestablish his or her identity so that a new and more stable relationship will develop. Most of this is still related to the marriage itself, either as an outright rejection of the values that the marriage seemed at first to have embodied, or as a continuation of the search for a life-partner that seemed to have been ended when the marriage began. Making sense of a divorce means rearranging many expectations. For instance, friends, or husbands of friends, suddenly declare how much they have fancied the new divorcée all the years that she was unavailable; they said nothing at the time, and she may fend them off, but it is tempting to give in just to have a pair of arms around her, and a warm body in what would otherwise be a comfortless bed. Many of these affairs will be with married people, and with the happily married ones who seem safer, and who will not fall in love and start another divorce epic rolling. The expectation that an ended marriage will be patched up often lingers through a series of half-committed affairs. Many of these affairs are warm and friendly and short-lived, and seem to do little harm. The longer affairs offer a kind of half-marriage, someone to care about and to stay alive for, yet an avoidance of real conflict and real passion. The divorced and widowed learn to make fools of themselves again, and to live with it. The greatest enemy is a runaway ideal that here at last is the one true lover, and that now all the hurt left over from the ended failure can be resolved and forgotten as if it never happened. The greatest loneliness comes from having nobody to talk to, not from having nobody to sleep with. But you may have to learn all over again how to talk, and how to listen, before you get things back into proportion. You have to make a new start, and the best way is to develop new skills, not merely to try to rediscover or re-deploy old skills.

Whether you have been married before or not, an affair with someone who is married is like most love affairs. Affairs make sense because they give people a chance to get to know each other intimately, and because they offer both partners a chance of regular sexual communication. Just as sexual communication in marriage helps the partners reduce tension between them, and reaffirm their value to each other by enabling each to confirm his value to himself, so it works also in an affair. Through sex the lovers can express and explore their need for each other, sharing together the secret and unique qualities of their personalities that would otherwise go unused and be meaningless. At its best, sex is a triumph of reality, not an escape into fantasy. It extends the boundaries of what we are. In a good marriage this process binds two people together day after day, week after week, year after year. In a good affair it can do the same, but there are impediments. The worst of these is the lack of time. Quarrels have to be settled at each visit. Hurts must be soothed before the married lover leaves. In an affair, the loving has to be timed and still be spontaneously given. Feelings must be dealt with as they appear, since they cannot be saved up for later, as they can in marriage. Lovers can too easily find that they spend most of their time being miserable about how little time they have, instead of using their time to the fullest.

If your husband or wife is having an affair

What are you to do? First, are you sure? In the end, there is only one thing to do if you are not sure, and that is to find out whether or not you want to be sure. Consider the position of the wife who suspects that her husband is having an affair. She can ask him outright. If he says yes, then she may not be able to cope with her own feelings, and he may be either unwilling or unable to help her do so. A marriage with its normal pleasures and problems may now seem to be over, and all the trust on which it was based seems shattered beyond repair. If he says no, and she has good reason to suspect that he is lying, she will be no better off. Perhaps he will be able to convince her otherwise, but this will only make it harder for him to tell her later if he does have an affair, and the cycle known as marital paranoia will start again. So it is not a question of being sure, but a matter of deciding whether you really want to know and why you want to know.

Often people want to know because they are afraid, and wish to express that fear, or because they feel angry and hurt, and want to be seen as angry and hurt. Everybody has the right to feel like this when a trust has been betrayed. The problem is that anger, fear, and pain are such powerful feelings that they work only through one-way communication. They destroy any possibility of two-way communication until they are brought under control once more, and by then the situation may have been altered by the destructive forces that were let loose. At the same time, people who are trying to control their anger and fear under these circumstances are almost bound to fail. Self-control breaks down. The bitterness shows. If we feel betrayed and jealous, it is almost impossible to contain these feelings and to be calm and rational about anything. The "wronged" wife or husband is caught in a trap. Is the answer to bottle up one's feelings with massive self-control, or is it to let rip and express all the feelings at once? The first course of action will probably fail, and the second will prevent two-way communication. Clearly, neither of these will work.

There are two ways around the problem. The first of these is to go one step at a time, and to allow the feelings to be dealt with at each step. If possible, husband and wife should take a step in turn. Both are going to be feeling strong and destructive emotions, and both need time to adjust to the new situation. This new situation, moreover, need not simply be the ruins of the old one. It can be something valuable in itself, worth having once the dust has settled. Once the question "Are you having an affair?" is asked, and the answer "Yes" has been reached, both partners need to pause and get used to the idea before any more questions are dealt with. This point can be made more clearly by looking at an imaginary dialogue. (Note: The roles are interchangeable. For "wife" you can read "husband.")

WIFE: Are you having an affair? (1)

HUSBAND: Why do you want (need) to know? (2)

WIFE: Because I wish to adjust to the realities of our marriage; because I feel hurt, angry, and afraid; and because I want to deal with those feelings first and bring them under control before deciding what to do. (3)

HUSBAND: Yes, I am having an affair. (4)

WIFE: I'm going to lose control of my feelings very soon, now. I have a right to do this, and nothing you can do will stop that. I need to know certain things about the affair, and these things are going to hurt me, but I have the deal with that hurt for myself. (5)

How long has it been going on? (6)

Is it serious? (*i.e.*, Does it mean that our marriage is over?) (7)

Who (if I don't know already) is it? (8)

The temptation is to skip several parts of this dialogue, and use only the parts numbered 1 and 4 before launching into a series of desperately hurtful questions beginning with 6, and going on to questions such as "How could you?" "Why didn't you tell me?" "What kind of a fool does this make me?" "What were you doing last Tuesday?" "How often do you see her?" "Is she better in bed than I am?" and so on. Usually, 2, 3, and 5 are unspoken verbally and expressed in other, non-verbal ways, but unless these points are communicated and agreed upon, there will be no dialogue at any safe level. Making these points allows the wife in the given script to take time to adjust her feelings, and also establishes that she has a right to express them. She needs to lose control, and to be given time to do so. When she launches herself into the next series of questions, this is because she has lost control. But sooner or later she will wish to re-establish communication, not as a hurt child, but as a wronged adult. The problem they both face is the need to let her do this in such a way that all the pent-up worry, when it comes out, does not trap her permanently into being a wronged child. If her husband is to succeed in his side of this strategy, he has to feel her pain too, and wait his turn. He had far longer than she to get used to the idea of his unfaithfulness, and he has already benefited from this at her expense. All he can do now is face his share in her pain, and feel it, and wait, doing nothing to make it worse, but not trying to make it better either. At this stage, it is probably best if he does not answer any more questions until she is calmer. "How could you?" must be answered eventually by the whole readjustment, which will take a long time. "Why didn't you tell me?" needs to be answered also by a total re-examination of the relationship. "What kind of a fool, etc.?" is a rhetorical question, to be answered only by those who ask it. "What were you doing on such-and-such an occasion?" reveals the web of lies and deceit woven to protect the affair, and will only hurt both deceiver and deceived. It has no relevance at this stage, since the fact of betrayal has to be faced as a whole, not in detail. "How often do you see her?" is also an irrelevant detail at this stage, and "Is she better in bed?" is a cry for reassurance that the victim would be in no position to use even if it were offered.

The wife in the dialogue faces an "intellectual" problem in addition to dealing with her own emotions. She has been deceived, and this means that many things she had judged one way have now turned out to be something else. She probably recognized signs and symptoms, but chose to deny to herself that they meant what she first thought. Perhaps she saw her husband and the other woman together, and wondered if there was anything going on between them. Most people have the skill to make sense of the behavior of other people: what it means when they look at each other a certain way, or stand close together. She will almost certainly have asked her husband, and been told a lie or half-truth designed to deceive. Now that she knows that she has been deceived over the affair as a whole, a great many things will need to be re-examined mentally and new judgments formed about what these things meant. For example, that vacation, or business trip, or weekend. Were they together? She cannot take more lies, or she will not know where she is. Yet so many things that puzzled her will make no sense at all.

She is therefore forced by her own state of mind into wishing to revise all her values at once. This is not humanly possible. They have to be revised a few at a time. Yet she cannot establish any order of priority. So she needs help, and has to ask for it. One way to do this is to allow her husband to express his priorities:

WIFE: I need help. We both do. What can I do to help you?

Whatever else the husband does at this point, he is forced to state his own priorities. He too has feelings that need to be dealt with inside the marital relationship. Least likely of all is that he wants to hurt his wife any further at this stage. Her calm in any case will only be temporary. So whatever he says forces him to reveal more things that she does not know, and to help her cope with his own feelings. It is his turn now to reveal any fear or anger or hurt, and to exercise his right to sound childish and illogical. "What can I do to help?" really means "What can I do to help you get your own feelings out in the open where you and I, not you and your lover, can start to work at them?" She is not condoning his actions, or condemning him for them, but trying to listen to him in a fresh way. What he will now say verbally is what he said before, both verbally and by his actions, except that when he said it before she could not hear him.

This strategy of "a little at a time" is one way to avoid the full destructive force of jealousy and hurt pride when an affair is revealed. It can be used in many ways, and the above dialogue is only one example. Essentially it works only to the extent that the feelings are dealt with as each new piece of hurtful information emerges, and are neither bottled up nor allowed to pile up into unmanageable proportions. In the throes of jealousy we alternate widely between self-disgust and disgust for the other person. Then, when the violence of the swing from one extreme to the other is blunted, the next step can be taken. This only works if there are a few hours available after the first question. If your spouse may be having an affair, and you are sure you want to know, first of all make an agreement to discuss the crisis as logically and as fairly as possible. Then set up a time to face the first hour or two together, without pressure of other appointments, children coming home from school, parents on the telephone for chatting, or people having to rush off for work in the middle of the crisis. It is best to allow three hours, even if the affair may be over, or nearly over, or not a serious threat to the marriage. Remember that all human behavior is based on skill, and that this requires practice, and that neither of you has done this before. You will not get it right at the first discussion, but you should give yourself the best chance of success.

There is another strategy available to you that works quite well for some people, and that is to take parental responsibility, as in the following imaginary dialogue:

> WIFE: I'd like to ask you something, and it's serious and will take time. Please sit down and listen, and don't say anything yet. I have been wondering lately if you are having an affair. Don't tell me, yet. If you are, then I want to get used to the idea, and if not, then something must be wrong between us. Now, what I want to ask is this: Can we set aside two or three hours to talk about ourselves and our relationship, and can we do it today?

To approach the problem in this way requires strength and preparation. Just discussing the matter with friends or parents can help. The method is based on two ideas. First, the intention is to regard the affair not as a cause of your difficulties but as a symptom. The relationship has not worked as well as you would have liked, and the affair you suspect to be taking place is probably only one indication of this fact. As a result, you are more alone than you wish to be. There has been a concealed withdrawal from the mutuality of your marriage, but there must also have been obvious and open forms of withdrawal—lack of time together, lack of sexual contact or interest, difficulties in agreeing over money or the house, arguments over the children or over contact with both or either of your families. In tackling causes, the main objective will be to review your marriage together, and to establish a better relationship. Acceptance of the fact of an affair will be part of this. If there was no affair, and your fears were groundless, the fact nevertheless that you suspected one shows a need for such a review. It will take time, and require a new set of skills that have to be developed as you go, in that both of you need to learn to express feelings that have been hidden before.

The second idea on which this approach is based is that when we establish communication with another person we often assume different roles, the three most important being "parent," "adult," and "child." Sometimes we trick people by approaching them as "adult" so that they are prepared to talk openly, but then we switch without warning into being the hurt or rebellious child. For example, if the wife in the imaginary dialogue says, "Can we talk about it seriously?" and her husband says, "Yes," she might then reply: "It's sure as hell time you talked to me about it. I'm always the last one you tell anything." In this way she alters the relationship and becomes a hurt and victimized child, incapable of talking about the real problem.

Good communication under stress requires a steady responsibility on both sides. The two people must use the part of their personality that cares about the other person as a wise parent would care, above the battle, not personally hurt by it except within the mature inner core of parental loneliness. The "child" about which they are concerned is their relationship. It is in trouble, and needs care and help, even if this means that it must, so to speak, grow up and leave them. The two people both want to know what went wrong—not in a spirit of anger and hurt pride to avenge the past, but to help the "child" grow up in safety and security, or to go happily and courageously if the time has come for it to die. Because we are not nowadays used to death, we are unpracticed at the death of our relationships. When a child is in poor health, we need to nurse and to love that child, to help it survive. If it may die, the fact has to be faced, in a caring way, not by hasty euthanasia.

If an affair matters to you, then the marriage matters also. To set aside time to discuss it may not be easy. However, this is far more important than the fact (or otherwise) of an affair. Indeed, an affair need not break up a marriage, and many couples survive the telling to go on to a new kind of relationship in which they recognize and respect the new growth in each other. Affairs happen in secret partly because one partner needs to grow privately. People can and do reach the limit of understanding about their partners. New people in their lives give them a chance to grow and to learn, to exercise curiosity, to be themselves in new ways. If you cannot tolerate this in your partner, then your parents may be to blame in the sense that they did not help you grow and learn, exercise curiosity, or be yourself, and, as a result, you can see no value in this. Yet, if you can tolerate it, you can learn from it too, as parents who are wise learn from their children, accepting that they are human themselves and have much to learn too.

The best preparation for all this—whether you are having a secret affair, as lover or spouse, or whether you are married to someone who might one day have an affair (and that is most of us)—is to develop healthy relationships. Love works for us all at an unconscious level, and the abuse of this word *unconscious* bedevils our understanding of the concept. Theoretically, "unconscious" is best thought of not as a great submerged tideway in our minds, a hidden and unpredictable set of forces that rule us against our will. The unconscious part of us is merely the store of experience within us that has survived from the past. When we were children our behavior helped us survive in the face of powerlessness to meet our own needs. All the survival behaviors we learned then are with us still. We use them in every waking moment. They are the unconscious. If we can accept that these behaviors helped as make sense of our childhood experience in often illogical ways, we can also accept that as grown-ups much of that behavior is now inappropriate. Love is illogical because the child is illogical, and because in matters of love we prefer to be children. We do not have to be the victims of unconscious motivation, however. In our love affairs we can use our maturity to learn what kind of a child we were, and to become a new kind of child, one who can feel and express delight and joy without guilt and fear. We can take over from the parents we had, and do a better job than they did. To have a successful affair, marital or extra-marital, we have to become more successful at being who we might have been, people who are more useful to others because they understand all the other lonely people.

Index

Adolescence, 35–37, 41, 162–63, 165, 175–76
Affairs (*see* Extra-marital affairs)
Age differences, 143–60
Alternative affairs, 13

Berne, Eric, 34
Birth, 1
Bisexuality, 129–42

Casual affairs, 6, 11, 30, 87–90, 111–22, 128, 180
Church weddings, 4
Civil-ceremony weddings, 4
Commitment, 11, 62
Communication, 58–60, 80, 187–93
Competitive "tit-for-tat" affair, 93–94
Computer-dating agencies, 170
Confession, 11
Conforming marriages, 37
Connivance, 104
Contraception, 5, 109
Control, emotional, 53–56, 80

Death, 1
Dependence, emotional, 32–39
Development, emotional, 32–39
Discovery of affair, 11, 53, 55–58, 63–81, 175–76, 187–93
Divorce, 11, 64, 161–62, 185
Double standard, 37, 104, 168, 182
Dowry system, 3

Economic factor in marriage, 19
Emotional control, 53–56, 80
Emotional dependence, 96, 97
Emotional development, 32–39
Escape motivation for marriage, 33–34
Exclusivity, sexual, 12, 20–23, 44, 166
Extended family, 3, 4, 5
Extra-marital affairs:
    alternative, 13
    attitudes of "other person," 105–10
    attitudes of spouse, 98–104
    attitudes toward, 5–6
    casual, 6, 11, 30, 87–90, 111–22, 128, 180

communication, 58–60, 80, 187–93
competitive "tit-for-tat," 93–94
continuing, 63–81
discovery of, 11, 53, 56–58, 63–81,
    175–76, 187–93
emotional control, 53–56, 80
fantasies, 26–28, 30
first, 12, 26–27, 31, 47–62, 178–79
guilt, 7, 10, 23, 24, 30, 34, 44, 85, 86,
    139, 171, 176, 179
homosexual, 129–42
incompatibility, 87
jealousy, 12, 46, 53, 60, 80, 190
justifications for, 82–110
middle age, 143–60
morality of, 161–71
multiple, 122–28, 177–78
nature of, 13–17
older–younger relationships, 143–60
one-night stands, 14, 30, 111–23, 128
opportunities for, 28–29
readiness for 26–46
realities of, 172–93
retaliatory, 17–18
as safety valve, 7
secrecy, 7–9, 11
significance of, 6–7
subsequent use of, 17–18
successful, 172–93
supplementary, 13
timing, 17
trial, 39–41

Family, importance of, 6
Fantasies, 26–28, 30
Fidelity, 12, 20–23, 44, 166, 167
First affairs, 12, 26–27, 31, 47–62,
    178–79
First marriages, 4
Forgiveness, 97–98, 102, 177
Friendship clubs, 170

Gossips, 9
Growing up, myths about, 34–39
Guilt, 7, 10, 23, 24, 30, 34, 44, 85, 86,
    139, 171, 176, 179

Homosexual affairs, 129–42

Ideal marriage, 18, 24–25
Illegitimate births, 4

Incompatibility, 87
Insecurity, 8–9

Jealousy, 12, 46, 53, 60, 80, 190

Kinsey Report, 30

Lesbians, 129–42
Love, 18, 19, 34, 44

Male menopause, 36
Male sterilization, 158
Marriages:
    age at, 4
    church weddings, 4
    conflict in, 2–3
    conforming, 37
    defense of, 168–69
    economic factor in, 19
    emotional development and, 32–39
    as escape, 33–34
    expectations and attitudes, 2–3, 6,
        18–25, 169–71
    fidelity, 12, 20–23, 44, 166, 167
    first, 4
    ideal, 18, 24–25
    love, 18, 19, 34
    open, 93
    partnership in, 18, 19
    popularity of, 2
    protection of, 7
    rates, 161
    (*see also* Extra-marital affairs)
Masturbation, 41, 134
Maternal love, 44
Media, 30
Ménage à trois, 20, 22, 58
Menopause, 35, 36, 148–49
Middle age, relationships during 143–60
Midlife crisis, 36
Morality, 161–71
Multiple affairs, 122–28, 177–78
Multiple marriages, 10

Older–younger relationships, 143–60
One and only love, myth of, 85–86
One-night stands, 14, 30, 111–23, 128
Open marriage, 93
Orgasm, 5, 24, 168, 169

Partnership in marriage, 18, 19
Pre-marital pregnancy, 4

Pre-marital sexual experience, 5
Premature ejaculation, 31
Privacy, 32

Remarriage, 2, 64, 149
Retaliatory affairs, 17–18
Romantic love, 19, 34
Rumors, 9

Sarcasm, 94
Secrecy, 7–9, 11
Self-control, 166, 187
Self-deceit, 83–84
Self-discipline, 25
Self-sacrifice, 90, 166, 167
Sex education, 30
Sex roles, 19
Sexual equality, 5
Sexual exclusivity, 12, 20–23, 44, 166, 167

Single people, 4, 11, 181–185
Sleeping Beauty myth, 34–35
Sterilization, male, 158
Supplementary affairs, 13

Timing, 17
Trial affairs, 39–41
Trust, 61, 96
Tweedie, Jill, 63

Unselfish love, 19

Vasectomy, 158
Venereal disease, 178
Virginity, 3, 4, 24, 100

Widows, 44, 185

Younger–older relationships, 143–60